History of the Good Intent Co-operative Society, Ltd., 1859-1909

With chapters on Robert Owen, G.J. Holyoake, the co-operative movement prior to 1859, and the cotton famine

J. H. Hinchcliffe

Alpha Editions

This edition published in 2019

ISBN : 9789353978020

Design and Setting By
Alpha Editions
email - alphaedis@gmail.com

As per information held with us this book is in Public Domain.
This book is a reproduction of an important historical work.
Alpha Editions uses the best technology to reproduce historical
work in the same manner it was first published to preserve its
original nature. Any marks or number seen are left intentionally
to preserve its true form.

HISTORY

OF THE

STALYBRIDGE GOOD INTENT

INDUSTRIAL

Co-operative Society Limited.

1859—1909.

With Chapters on Robert Owen, G. J. Holyoake, the Co-operative Movement prior to 1859, and the Cotton Famine.

BY

J. H. HINCHLIFFE,
General Secretary to the Society.

MANCHESTER:
CO-OPERATIVE PRINTING SOCIETY LIMITED, 118, CORPORATION STREET.

1909.

PREFACE.

WHEN the Jubilee Committee asked me to undertake the writing of this history, I suggested that I should make a better editor than author, and gave expression to a fear that the book would be a very thin one if left entirely to me. Their answer was, in effect, that the history of Stalybridge Co-operative Society required more at my hands than editing, and here it is. I still thought that the words should be largely those of others, hence the moderately full reports of addresses of men who attended the early gatherings.

It is thought that the chapters preceding those of the movement in our own town will prepare the reader, and particularly the younger reader, for a better understanding of the ups and downs of the early years. The person, for instance, who knew nothing of the cotton famine could scarcely appreciate the self-denying efforts of the steadfast co-operators who stuck to their society during the trying years 1861 to 1865.

My acknowledgments are due first of all to Mr. Edwin Wright, the society's cashier, whose ability as a shorthand writer has been of great service. He not only writes phonography himself, but transcribes my shorthand notes accurately. Thus, reading each others' notes, we have obtained much information that might, without his assistance, have been missed.

The staff of Messrs. J. Andrew and Company, of the *Reporter* Office, Ashton-under-Lyne, has been most helpful and obliging in placing at our disposal files of the *Reporter*, from which valuable reports of the early meetings, extracts from the society's accounts, and comments have been obtained.

My thanks are also due to Mr. J. H. Milligan, Central grocery manager, whose recollection of the doings and the people of many years ago is so vivid ; and to Mr. Charles Wright, manager of Manchester and Salford Society, who in 1907 revealed a remarkable knowledge of the operations some 48 years before of our pioneers at Stalybridge. When Mr. Wright was approached he gave hints as to sources of information, and himself sent valuable copy, which, together with his cheery manner, was a great help.

Mr. Richard Baxter, son of our first secretary, very readily lent a number of his late father's papers, including several letters from the Rochdale Pioneers' Society received in 1859 and 1860.

Mrs. Worsley (*née* Miss Hampshire) gave useful information as to drapery in the early days, and kindly lent the photograph of the staff in the early 'seventies.

Other acknowledgments are due to members of the staff, particularly to Mr. Ernest Lees, for their putting me in touch with others connected with the society many years ago ; and to Mr. T. Emmett, photographer,

who turned up negatives by his late father and himself.
The portraits are from photographs almost entirely the
work of Mr. Emmett.

I am indebted, too, to the authors and editors of the
following books, &c., for much useful information :—

Mr. C. W. F. Goss's " Bibliography of the Writings of George
Jacob Holyoake." This work involved the reading by him of
some 400 books. When permission was sought, Mr. Goss
replied : " Take whatever you desire."

Mr. Lloyd Jones' " Life and Times of Robert Owen."

Mr. G. J. Holyoake's " History of Co-operation."

The " History of the Rochdale Pioneers," by the same author.

" Industrial Co-operation," edited by Catherine Webb.

" Industrial History of England," by H. de B. Gibbins,
Litt.D., M.A.

" Short History of English Commerce," by L. L. Price.

" Our Story," published by the Co-operative Union Limited.

The " Co-operative Wholesale Societies' Annual."

The *Co-operative News.*

" Bygone Stalybridge," by Samuel Hill, printed by Messrs.
Geo. Whittaker and Sons.

" A. L." in the *Manchester Evening News* of October 14th,
1908.

" A Visit to Lancashire in December, 1862," by Ellen Barlee.

J. H. HINCHLIFFE.

CONTENTS.

PART I.

CHAPTER I
PAGE
The hard lot of the Workers at the end of the 18th Century and the beginning of the 19th—The First Factory Act—Robert Owen 19

CHAPTER II.
George Jacob Holyoake.............................. 25

CHAPTER III.
Co-operation prior to 1859.......................... 32

CHAPTER IV.
The Cotton Famine.................................. 36

PART II.

CHAPTER I.
The Start at Stalybridge 47

CHAPTER II.
The Opening in Water Street........................ 60

CHAPTER III.
The First Tea Party................................. 71

CHAPTER IV.
Another Year's Work—Four Branches Opened—A Year's Sales £42,114—1862 Annual Meeting—Effect of Cotton Panic—Co-operation in Stalybridge on its Trial...... 83

CHAPTER V.
Dissension—Resignation of Officers—Struggling Departments—Society owns a Dog—Rumours circulated by Opponents—Vote of Confidence.................... 90

CONTENTS. 13

CHAPTER VI.—1863-4.   PAGE

Sales still Lower, but a Better Balance Sheet—1s. 6d.
Dividend—Education and *The Co-operator*—No Dividend—A Crowded Meeting—Business Transferred to Grosvenor Street—Members of Committee Resign—Proposal to Buy Property—Butchering Given Up—One Grocer's and One Draper's Shop only left....... 101

CHAPTER VII.—1865.

Influence of Cotton Panic still evident—Co-operation's "Hour of Need"—Losses—Many Steadfast Members—Again a Shilling Dividend—Two Shops Owned—The Dark Days Passing.......................... 114

CHAPTER VIII.—1866 to 1868.

Steady Progress—Interesting Addresses by the Revs. J. P. Hopps and J. R. Stephens—Shares at Par—Shopmen's Bonus System—Tailoring Agencies taken up—Represented at Annual Conference—*Reporter* Account of Chequered Career and the Great Change—Mr. J. Ridgway becomes Treasurer 123

CHAPTER IX.—1869 to 1874.

Large Gathering of Members and Friends—Other Tailoring Agencies—Making known the *Co-operative News*—Mr. Greenwood Retires—Mr. P. H. Robinson and Mr. F. R. Beeley Appointed—Miss Hampshire Retires—Miss Woolley Appointed—The Society becomes a Member of the Co-operative Wholesale Society...... 136

CHAPTER X.—1874 to 1880.

Central Premises Extension—Mr. Seth Charlesworth, Secretary—Copper Pound Checks—Mr. J. Mellor Appointed Manager—High Street Branch Opened—Steam Power—Corn Mill Shares—Reserve Fund £1,000—Committee and Staff together at Tea—Existing Millbrook Branch Opened—Quarterly Conference Entertained—Loan Account—A Start in the Boot Trade—Coffee Roasting—Excursions................ 150

CONTENTS.

CHAPTER XI.—1881 to 1884.

Stalybridge Cotton Mill Shares—No. 3 Branch—Three Shillings Dividend—£50,000 Sales—Thomas Hughes Testimonial—Extension of High Street Branch—Manchester Royal Eye Hospital—Hebden Bridge Fustian Society—Crookbottom Company—Extension, Back Grosvenor Street—Large Gathering, 1884—First Advance on House Property—Huddersfield Road Branch—Coal Trade Commenced.................. 168

CHAPTER XII.—1885 to 1894.

Boots separated from Drapery—Manchester Ship Canal—Subscription to Co-operative Union—Book Check System Adopted—A Step Forward in Millinery and Dressmaking—Coal Wagons Bought—Stables Erected—Education Fund—Newsroom Opened and Closed—Fire—Butchering Again—Mr. F. E. Maden, Drapery Manager—Electric Light—3,000 Members—Heyrod Branch Opened—Mr. J. Green takes in hand Tailoring—Distress in Cotton Trade; Weekly Grants—First Soirée 184

CHAPTER XIII.—1894 to 1899.

Mr. J. H. Hinchliffe, Secretary—Mr. J. B. Mason, Manager—Members visit the "Wholesale"—Other Excursions—Concerts—Electric Lighting Extended—Cheetham Hill Road Property—Buckley Street Property—Lord Street Property—Wakefield Road, Heyrod, Property—Additional Stables—Building Rules—Infirmary Cot—Indian Famine Funds—Mill Operatives' Distress Fund—Engineers' Lockout Fund—West of Ireland Distress Fund—Small Savings Bank—First Exhibition—Castle Hall Branch—Telephone—Technical School—South African War Fund—Helping Reservists' Dependents—Volunteers' Prize Fund—Death of Mr. John Heap 203

CONTENTS. 15

CHAPTER XIV.—1900 to 1907. PAGE

Cheetham Hill Road Branch—" Climax " Check System—Work for Trade-unionists only—Spectacles Agency—Manchester Royal Infirmary—Children's Hospital—Society for Prevention of Cruelty to Children—Children's Gala—Millinery in Melbourne Street—Six Figures of Sales—Increased Production—Death of Mr. Samuel Knight—Abattoir—Defence Fund—Borough Education Committee—Excursion to London—Death of Mr. Wm. Hall—Cotton Shortage and Decrease in Turnover—Cotton Growing Association—Convalescent Homes—Another Local Distress Fund—Delegates—Office of Treasurer Abolished—Sundries Society Directorate—Printing Society Shares—Corn Mills taken over by the Wholesale Society—Premier Mills—Electric Motors—Knitting Machinery—Mr. J. T. Bate Resigns—President a Magistrate—Bookkeeping Class—Miss Firth, Milliner—Miss Holt, Dressmaker—Interest on Shares 219

CHAPTER XV.—1907 to 1909.

Union New Headquarters—What the Co-operative Union has done—Sundries Society's New Works—C.W.S. Bank Account—Adding by Machinery—" Our Circle "—Death of Mr. J. Bailey—Sales £129,537—Committee Elections—Canvassing—Co-operative Insurance Society—Ashton District Infirmary—Death of Mr. Thomas Knott—Castle Hall Mill Bought—Story of Drapery continued—Mr. T. Faulkner, Drapery Manager—Stocks Branch, No. 8—Sundries Society Shares and Loan—Collective Insurance—Jubilee Committee 233

PART III.

Jubilee Celebration 249
Conclusion 285

APPENDIX.

Past and Present Officers........................... 287
Members and Sales at Different Periods.............. 291
Balance Sheet as at 5th June, 1909.................. 292
Sales, Dividend, and Interest since the Start........... 292

ILLUSTRATIONS.

	PAGE
President, Secretary, and Manager	3
General Committee	5
Jubilee Committee	7
Former Members of Committee	145, 165, 179, 207
Committee, 1862 to 1864	91
Auditors, Treasurers, and Solicitors	227
Managers of Departments	185
Managers, Central Grocery and Branches	155
Former Officials	151
The Staff in the Early 'Seventies	141
Central Grocery	109
Central Butchering	193
Drapery, Dressmaking, and Millinery	239
Tailoring	201
Boot Department	187
No. 1 Branch—High Street	157
No. 2 Branch—Millbrook	161
No. 3 Branch—Mount Pleasant	169
No. 4 Branch—Huddersfield Road	181
No. 5 Branch—Heyrod	197
No. 6 Branch—Castle Hall	211
No. 7 Branch—Cheetham Hill Road, Dukinfield	221
No. 8 Branch—Taylor Street, Stocks Lane	243

PART I.

CHAPTER I.

THE HARD LOT OF THE WORKERS—THE FIRST FACTORY ACT—
ROBERT OWEN.

THE lot of the workers at the end of the 18th century and in the early part of the 19th was a hard one. In 1802 the first Factory Act was passed at the instance of Sir Robert Peel. It was described as an Act " for the preservation of the health and morals of apprentices and others employed in cotton and other mills." The immediate cause of the Bill was the fearful spread through the factory districts of Manchester of epidemic disease, owing to the overwork, scanty food, wretched clothing, long hours, bad ventilation, and overcrowding in unhealthy dwellings of the workpeople, especially the children. The hours of work were reduced to 12 per day, but the Act did not apply to children residing near the factory in which they were employed, for they were supposed to be under the supervision of their parents. In his " Industrial History of England," Mr. H. de B. Gibbins says: " We hear of children and young people in factories

CO-OPERATION IN STALYBRIDGE.

overworked and beaten as if they were slaves;" and Southey, writing in 1833, said of factory labour that the slave trade was mercy compared to it.

To Robert Owen is due the credit of being the originator of co-operation. He was born in 1771, at the commencement of the new system of industrial life. The factory system took the place of the domestic, and the conditions of labour were entirely changed. The people whose labour was rapidly displaced by machinery could not so rapidly adapt themselves to the new conditions, and there was deep poverty and severe suffering. This was the problem that faced Robert Owen, and in an endeavour to solve it he spent his life. He saw the danger lurking in the discontent of the people with regard to the apportionment of the wealth of the country, and he set himself to do what he could to avoid that danger. He devoted his time, money, and energy to the education and welfare of the people from whom co-operators sprang, with the result that in later years it became very much easier to co-operate. He had lived amongst the people, and knew what they suffered, and he made it his chief aim to ameliorate, as far as he could, their lot. He suffered for his efforts; derision and scoffing came to him, but he never turned aside.

After occupying situations in large drapery businesses, including one in St. Ann's Square, Manchester, and being a partner of a concern which made what were called mules, he became a manufacturer of fine yarn, first as an individual employer and afterwards as partner in a larger concern, and was regarded as one of the best judges of cotton in the market.

CO-OPERATION IN STALYBRIDGE.

How to get the most out of the machinery of Watt, Arkwright, Crompton, and others became the first consideration of the majority of the cotton manufacturers, and the factory system was pushed to extremes. By means of the Factory Acts and in other ways much has been done to remove those evils, and the lot of the present-day mill worker is a happy one indeed compared with that of the worker in the same position in Owen's days.

On the 1st January, 1800, he commenced operations as a cotton manufacturer at New Lanark, Scotland, and at once commenced an experiment for the improvement of the condition of the workers, his aim being not to be a manager of cotton mills only, but to change the circumstances by which the people were surrounded, and which were so injurious to them. By the directions of Mr. Dale before him the pauper children working at the mills, who were in those days brought in large numbers from other parishes and housed in sheds, had been well lodged, fed and clothed; but Owen decided that no more pauper children should be received. He also determined that the village streets should be improved, and that better houses should be built to receive families to fill the places of the pauper children. There was at that time little if any protection of the workers by the law, but Owen did so much for them that differences arose between his partners and him, who thought he was expending too great a portion of the profits in that direction. He found a ruinous system of credit in operation, the small shopkeepers buying and selling on credit at high prices. He opened stores; bought for cash and sold at cost, at a saving to the people, it is said, of 25 per cent. The distrust of the workpeople was gradually removed, and when Owen, although he had to close the mills in consequence of the embargo placed by the United States on the export of raw cotton, paid them full wages for nearly four months, their complete confidence was gained. In spite of the opposition of his partners, who were in two cases bought out, he had schools erected, and although the cost per child was about £2 per year, the parents were charged only 3s. per year, the firm paying the difference. At twelve years of age the children could be sent into the works to contribute to the support of the family. He met opposition not only from his partners, but from other factory owners, and even from the clergy, the latter seeming to think that his efforts in the direction of education were an interference in their province. Others regarded the intellectual advancement of the workpeople as a political danger, and there was a risk of reform being denounced as an effort to upset the throne, attack property, and overthrow religion. Lloyd Jones, the author of "The Life and Times of Robert Owen," says, however, that in the matter of education for the people Owen was successful beyond his most sanguine expectations, and that there is every reason to believe that his last partners were thoroughly satisfied with his management as an employer of labour and a maker of profit, the profit realised being more than the deed of partnership required. The villagers presented a written address to the partners, thanking them for the many advantages enjoyed and expressing a desire that all cotton spinners might enjoy the same advantages.

CO-OPERATION IN STALYBRIDGE. 23

One of the strongest arguments for the existence of our co-operative movement is found in the opposition of Owen's partners to his efforts on behalf of the people. The partners were so afraid that their profits might be reduced that they forced a dissolution of partnership. Yet his management of the New Lanark Mills was so successful that, after paying 5 per cent on the capital employed, the net profit was at the rate of £40,000 a year. What an immense amount of good for the people might have been done had that profit been devoted to the purposes of the many, instead of taken by the few.

As showing the disinterestedness of the man, it may be mentioned that the meetings held in London for the fighting of the cause of the factory children cost him £4,000. He purchased thirty thousand extra copies of papers containing the reports, and had copies sent to the ministers of all the parishes in the kingdom, and to all members of both Houses of Parliament.

It is related elsewhere that in 1829 there were established 130 co-operative societies, and that by the end of 1831, although the exact number cannot be given, there were about 250 societies. The work of Robert Owen had prepared the way for their establishment, and although most of them went out of existence, they in turn had prepared the way for such societies as ours, on the Rochdale system. As Lloyd Jones puts it, it constitutes a special claim on our gratitude that Robert Owen brought into practical activity for the public good the energies of the humblest and poorest to augment the vast popular power by which the present co-operative movement is sustained. He laboured for the people ; he died working for them ; and his last thought was for their welfare. He was laid to rest within a short distance of his birthplace, in 1858.

In October, 1908, the Co-operative Wholesale Society held an exhibition at Newtown of co-operative productions, to commemorate the fiftieth anniversary of the death of Robert Owen. A few years before appreciation in a tangible form had been shown. Opposite the house wherein he was born stands a public library, and a tablet indicates that the Co-operative Union, acting on behalf of the societies of the country, was by far the largest donor to the building fund. A portion of the building is dedicated to his memory, another tablet making that fact known. Co-operators have also erected a memorial over the grave in Newtown churchyard, and it has been placed in the care of the local society by the Co-operative Union.

CHAPTER II.

G. J. HOLYOAKE.

AS the life and work of Robert Owen had such an influence in the direction of co-operation as we know it, so, it is thought, should any history of the co-operative movement, whether in a town or over the world, include more than a passing mention of the later work of G. J. Holyoake.

He was born in Birmingham on the 13th April, 1817, in days of social ferment. A commercial panic had reduced his parents from comparative comfort to anxious privation. His mother was a deeply religious woman, and brought up the boy very carefully. At the Sunday School he was considered so extremely pious that he was called "The angel child." He began his business career in days when labour was absolutely at the mercy of capital, and when it was almost a social misdemeanour for a working man to take an active part in politics. Before he was seven years of age he worked in a business conducted by his mother, and at nine he commenced regular work as a whitesmith. The impression he received while working at the foundry, of the petty tyranny of masters and the apathy and helplessness of workmen, played no small part in shaping his career. He came under the influence of Robert Owen in 1837, and in consequence of the bitterness of the clergy towards Owen and those who held his views, and because of their accusations of heresy, was led to taking sides with free-thought. During the same year he began his advocacy of co-operation. With three fellow students of the Mechanics' Institute he formed a small Utopian community, and they all four lived together in an " associated house." What these young men advocated on a large scale they sought to practise on a small one, on the principle that one should do what one could, when unable to do what one would.

Mr. Holyoake associated with the Chartists immediately after the passing of the Reform Bill, when he was but 15 years of age ; but, although a Chartist and frequently acting with the party, he never joined in their war upon the Whigs. He even published a criticism of Chartism, in which he suggested that violent action was altogether unnecessary, and he became an exponent of the best aspirations of the working classes. He became an uncompromising foe of churches and churchmen, and that attitude was mainly due to the relentlessness with which the Church persecuted unfriended free-thought, and the harsh legality by which it gathered taxes from the very poor of the parish in which he lived. One of his earliest memories was of a time when his parents were struggling to keep the wolf from the door and his little sister fell dangerously ill, sadly needing all the nourishments that could be afforded. The money laid aside for the church rate or Easter dues had to be expended on suitable food for the sick child. Within a few days the rector issued a summons, and dreading the possible warrant of distraint, such as had been served upon a neighbour, the mother took the money herself, none of the children being old enough, to pay the dues. She was kept waiting at the court five or six hours until the case was called, and when she returned the child was a corpse. So very dear was this young sister to him that from the moment of her death he unconsciously turned his heart to methods of secular deliverance. Mr. Holyoake has been described as an atheist ; Mr. C. W. F. Goss, author of the admirable bibliography of the writings of G. J. Holyoake, says he was not an atheist, although he was wholly for the right of atheism, or any other opinion that appealed to reason to be heard.

In 1845 the Manchester Unity of Oddfellows offered five prizes of £10 each for five new lectures on Charity, Truth, Knowledge, Science, and Progression, to be read to members of the order in taking successive degrees. There were 79 competitors, some of them clergymen, and Mr. Holyoake, taking for his motto " *Justitia Sufficit*," was awarded the whole of the five prizes. The lectures were sanctioned by the Bristol A.M.C. in June, 1846, and published. They are still used.

He was one of the most earnest advocates of the repeal of the taxes on knowledge. One of his experiences was to be sued by the Government for publishing newspapers on unstamped paper. Early in the 'thirties the price of a newspaper was 7d., including the 4d.

revenue tax. In 1836 it was reduced by 3d., and in 1849 Mr. Holyoake became one of the active and enterprising members of an association formed to secure the exemption of the Press from all taxation. Each copy of a paper sold without a stamp involved a fine of £20 and possible imprisonment, and it is said that he incurred penalties to the extent of £600,000. The Treasury authorities appealed to Mr. Gladstone, whose reply was that he knew Mr. Holyoake's object was not to break the law but to test it, and who shortly afterwards repealed the taxes which fettered the Press. The repeal of the Act caused the prosecution to be abandoned.

The first part of the history of co-operation in Rochdale, 1844-1857, written by Mr. Holyoake, was issued in 1858 under the title "Self-Help by the People." The book was reproduced in every European language, while in England it was the seed from which sprang 250 co-operative societies in two years. Later a second part was added, and the whole published in one volume entitled " History of the Rochdale Pioneers." This has been reprinted three times, the last issue being dated 1907.

In 1868 he became editor and joint proprietor of the *Social Economist*, which was, with true co-operative spirit, suspended in order that the *Co-operative News* might be the collective organ of co-operation.

His greatest literary work for the movement, however, is the "History of Co-operation," commenced in 1873. The first volume was published in 1875 and the second in 1879. A revised and completed edition was published in 1906 by T. Fisher Unwin. Mr. Holyoake wrote the history of the great Leeds Industrial Co-operative Society, a society of 48,000 members, which completed its fiftieth year in 1897. In that book he writes : " I knew co-operation when it was born. I stood by its cradle. In every journal, newspaper, and review with which I was connected I defended it in its infancy when no one thought it would live For years I was its sole friend and representative in the press." At the advanced age of 85 he performed the ceremony of unveiling a monument over the grave of Robert Owen in Newtown churchyard.

In 1902 Mr. Holyoake defended the cause of co-operation against the private traders. The traders had adopted their boycotting tactics in St. Helens and other towns, in many cases getting people dismissed from employment solely because they were members of co-operative societies, and he wrote a series of ten papers for the *Co-operative News* in answer to the tradesmen's arguments. They were afterwards published in a volume entitled " Anti-boycott Papers."

He was a close friend of such men as Garibaldi, Emerson, John Bright, Richard Cobden, John Stuart Mill, W. E. Gladstone, and many others. His personal qualities were honesty, love of truth, charity, sympathy, unvarying good nature, and fairness towards his fellows and towards his foes. Mr. Cobden said he was the man to say the most unpleasant thing in the least unpleasant way. Almost the whole of his life he laboured for the cause of social reform and to ameliorate the condition of his fellows, and as an advocate for co-operation he helped to bring greater comfort and happiness to the operative classes and to provide working men with better homes, better wages, better food, and better opportunities for the educating of their children. He died in 1906.

There was a unanimous resolution at the Birmingham Congress in 1906, that the life and work of the late G. J. Holyoake and his services to the co-operative movement be perpetuated by a building bearing his name, to be erected as a habitation for the headquarters of the movement, in which facilities may be found for carrying on all kinds of work for the spread of co-operative ideals. On May 12th, 1908, more than the sum asked for had been promised, societies totalling 2,332,754 members having undertaken to contribute £24,667.

The last rites were observed at the Crematorium at Golders Green on Saturday, January 27th, 1906, and every public movement with which Mr. Holyoake had been actively associated paid its tribute of respect. A memorial sermon preached by the Rev. Dr. Clifford described Mr. Holyoake as a soldier of freedom, one fitted to take his place in the great company of the prophets of freedom and the apostles of liberty. He (the preacher) had no hesitation in placing him in the ranks of that great succession where they found Moses, who led the people into the land of promise, and of Judas Maccabæus, with the hammer of God that broke in pieces the tyranny of monarchs. He was in line with English leaders—Alfred, who fought against the oppression of the Danes, and Cromwell, who fought against tyranny in the name of religion. He had freed the press; he was a soldier of liberty. Joseph Cowen had said, with reference to the people who talked

CO-OPERATION IN STALYBRIDGE.

glibly about his religion, that he knew Christian people who would not go across the street to help another, but that Mr. Holyoake would go to any trouble to do a kindness. In fact, he was a much better Christian than many who made a loud profession of religion. " By their fruits ye shall know them."

  Thou glorious Titan, art thou gone at last ?
   Shall the embattled peal thy name no more ?
   Must the majestic spirit that of yore
  Made thy young heart a home be now outcast ?
  Ah, never ! with thy passing hath not passed
   The Truth eternal that thou suffer'dst for.
   Never again shall clang the iron door
  Thy bleeding hands thrust open and held fast.
   Servant of man, well done ! The great unborn
  Shall thunder forth thine honour in that light
   Whose radiant and unutterable morn
  Thy life hath hastened over Freedom's night.
   And o'er the upward pathway thou hast worn
  Thy steadfast name shall blaze, a star of might.
      EDEN PHILLPOTTS, in the *Tribune*.
February, 1906.

CHAPTER III.

CO-OPERATION PRIOR TO 1859.

MR. HOLYOAKE defines co-operation as "voluntary concert, with equitable participation and control among all concerned in any enterprise." As the same author says, it has been common since the commencement of human society in the sense of two or more persons uniting to attain an end which each could not attain singly.

Mr. Owen had pointed out that one oven might suffice to bake for a hundred families with little more cost and trouble of attendance than a single household involved, and set free a hundred fires and a hundred domestic cooks. Co-operative laundries were unknown in his days, but he suggested that one commodious wash-house and laundry would save one hundred disagreeable, screaming, steaming, toiling wash days in the homes of the people. And so could one large shop supersede twenty smaller shops and effect an enormous saving in administration.

As a result of Robert Owen's activities many

CO-OPERATION IN STALYBRIDGE.

societies, originally called union shops, were formed. At the end of 1829 the number of societies was 130 ; in 1831 they had increased to 250 ; and two years later there were 400. They divided profits, not according to purchases, but as interest on capital.

The first co-operative shop known in England was that of a tailoring society in Birmingham in 1777, and the second a store at Mongewell, Oxfordshire, in 1794.

Amongst others, in a list of early societies and their dates of establishment, the following local names appear :—Ashton, 1838 ; Broadbottom, 1831 ; Hyde, between 1830 and 1833 ; Macclesfield, 1829 ; Mottram, about 1830 ; Mossley, about 1830 ; and Stockport, 1839.

Most of the 400 societies referred to went out of existence, some for want of legal protection against unscrupulous members, others from the apathy of members and the fact that working people had not acquired the habit of association. The Combination Laws, consolidated in 1799 and 1800, regulated the price of labour and the relations between masters and workmen, and prohibited the latter from combining for their own protection. They were repealed in 1825.

It was left to the Rochdale Pioneers in 1844 to inaugurate a new era. The principle of dividend on purchases was in operation with a society at Meltham Mills, near Huddersfield, as early as 1827. It is also claimed to have been recommended by Mr. Alexander Campbell at Glasgow in 1822, and at Rochdale in 1840. It is believed, however, that the idea was separately originated by Mr. Charles Howarth, one of the 28 pioneers of Rochdale.

CO-OPERATION IN STALYBRIDGE.

A few days before Christmas, 1843, a few poor weavers, out of work and almost without food, met to discuss their condition and to make an effort to better it. They would become merchants and manufacturers on their own account. A subscription list was handed round, and a dozen of those present promised a weekly contribution of 2d. each. Three collectors called at the homes of the members for the subscriptions, walking miles for the collection of a few shillings. Other meetings were held; it was decided to open a co-operative provision store, and their society was registered as the "Rochdale Society of Equitable Pioneers" on the 24th October, 1844. The ground floor of a warehouse in Toad Lane was taken; Mr. William Cooper was appointed cashier—his duties were very light at first, says Mr. Holyoake; and Mr. Samuel Ashworth became salesman. The stock consisted of infinitesimal quantities of flour, butter, sugar, and oatmeal, of a total value of about £14. On the 21st December, 1844, they commenced business. A few of the co-operators, continues Mr. Holyoake, had clandestinely assembled to witness their own *dénouement*; and there they stood, like the conspirators under Guy Fawkes in the Parliamentary cellars, debating on whom should devolve the taking down of the shutters. One bold fellow rushed at it, and in a few minutes Toad Lane was in a titter, the "doffers" ventilating their opinions at the top of their voices and calling "Aye! th' owd weavers' shop is opened at last." A few women went in to ask for things they knew they could not get, just to look round and be able to report to others on the commodities for sale and at the bareness of the shelves.

It was declared that the shop would not be open a week.

But those pioneers had their reward. It remained open, and soon they were in a position to pay interest on capital and dividend on purchases. To what great things has that twopenny subscription led. From that timid beginning they have gone on until their members number 16,000, with a share capital of £314,000. They employ 370 people, pay £23,000 a year in wages, and their sales for a year amount to £350,000.

CHAPTER IV.

THE COTTON FAMINE.

There's a moan on the gale, there's a cry in the air,
'Tis the wail of distress, 'tis the sigh of despair ;
All silent and hushed is the factory's whirl,
And famine and want their black banner unfurl
Where the warm laugh of childhood is hushed on the ear,
And the glance of affection is met by the tear ;
Where hope's lingering embers are ready to die,
And utterance is chok'd by the heartbroken sigh.
   From " A Visit to Lancashire in December, 1862,"
     By ELLEN BARLEE.

THE supply of cotton from North America nearly ceased in consequence of the secession of the Southern States from the Union in 1860-61. At the beginning of the latter year the prospect seemed to the operatives so bright that they pressed for an advance in wages. In March there was a turn-out of weavers at several mills. Somewhat suddenly the American Civil War broke out, and at once it was realised that the mills must close for want of cotton unless the war came to an end soon. The weavers returned to work after a brief struggle, but the war continued and the mills were run short time. Some were closed altogether, and the operatives, with aching hearts, became unwilling recipients of relief. "Short commons and long faces," said one, were his recollections of the "panic." "I wur nobbut a lad at th' time, but I'd a lad's keen feelin's, especially in certain vital parts. I wur punced through th' panic, I wur."

So scarce did employment become that in the winter of 1862-3 nearly 7,000 of 11,484 operatives usually employed were out of work, and a large number of those employed were on short time. Of 39 cotton manufactories, 24 foundries and machine shops, and three bobbin turning shops in the town, only five were employed full time with all hands; 17 full time with a reduced number of hands; 34 on short time; and seven were stopped. A gigantic system of relief was organised in the town, and it is said that more than three-fourths of the population became dependent. The cotton operatives were not so well organised as now, and what little they had saved was soon exhausted. Contributions of money, immense quantities of clothing, and cloth for making up flowed in from all parts of England. To provide food for the distressed people orders on grocers in the town were issued. To clothe them the garments received from various parts were distributed, and the tailors of the town were employed by the relief committee to make up the cloth. When that work was done many of the tailors went to the workhouse, some to repair the clothing of the inmates, and some to become inmates themselves. The Rev. Mr. and Mrs. Hoare started a school in the Albion Mills, employing a tailor to teach the men who attended to mend their own clothing. Another considerate action of Mr. Hoare's was to forego his fees for marriages solemnised at St. Paul's. Mr. James Buckley, of Buckley and Newton's, was a generous helper. It is said that he told the people, "You'll never starve so long as you have plenty of bacon and potatoes," and he gave large quantities of those comestibles. About the beginning of 1863 our society distributed quantities of stew from the butchering department.

Mr. B. Worth had the shop at the end of Castle Street. On one occasion a mob of half-famished people went for it, but Mr. Worth was prepared. He announced that if they would come at ten o'clock the next morning he would distribute 200 loaves. The crowd passed on; at the appointed time the loaves were thrown from the windows and caught by the people.

Sewing schools were opened for the women and girls, who were paid for attending, and instructed in dressmaking and other sewing work each afternoon, and in ordinary school subjects in the morning. These are referred to in Sam Laycock's "Sewin' Class Song"—

> Come, lasses, let's cheer up an' sing;
> It's no use lookin' sad;
> We'll mak' our sewin' schoo' to ring,
> An' stitch away like mad.
> We'll try an' mak' th' best job we con
> O' owt we han to do;
> We read, an' write, an' spell, an' keawnt,
> While here at th' sewin' schoo'.

> Sin' th' war began, an' th' factories stopped,
> We're badly off, it's true,
> But still we needn't grumble,
> For we'n noan so mich to do;
> We're only here fro' nine to four,
> An' han an hour for noon;
> We noather stop so very late,
> Nor start so very soon.

CO-OPERATION IN STALYBRIDGE. 39

One rather humorous local incident may be remembered by some readers. Mr. Bates' mill in Castle Street was used as one of the relief stores. A man stationed at the door for the purpose of regulating the applicants had a way of issuing the command " Hook it ! " to any applicant who became importunate. The expression stuck to the man the rest of his life, and after his death people were asked, " Do'st know ' Hook-it's ' dead ? "

Another, a retired army sergeant, marched out numbers of the unemployed men and put them through exercises ; anything to keep them occupied.

The decision of the relief committee to issue tickets instead of money resulted in the " Bread Riots." The great excitement commenced on the morning of Thursday, March 19th, 1863, when the executive committee sent word to the schools that relief would be given by ticket at the rate of 3s. a week, but that a day in hand would be kept. The scholars objected. They contended that they ought to receive their " wages " in money and to the full amount, or attend what they termed the labour test certain hours per week less. The tickets were refused, and a vast crowd congregated around Castle Street Mill. The windows of a cab in which Mr. Bates and Mr. J. Kirk were riding had its windows smashed, portions of the mill machinery were broken, and missiles were thrown at the police, who had turned out under the superintendence of Mr. Wm. Chadwick, chief constable. The officers were quite overpowered by the mob, which numbered hundreds. Much damage was done to shops in Market Street, particularly those occupied by Mr. Brierley, the druggist, and Mr. Dyson, the eating-house keeper, and the shopkeepers were soon busy putting up their shutters. The animus of the mob seemed to be directed, however, toward the more prominent members of the relief committee. At Mr. Bates' house, in Cockerhill, windows were broken and many valuable pieces of furniture destroyed, even young women joining in the wanton destruction. From there the mob turned again to Market Street, Melbourne Street, and Caroline Street. Every window of the Central Relief Committee rooms in Melbourne Street was smashed. At the shop of Mr. Ashton, another member of the relief committee, bottles, canisters, and groceries were thrown about and destroyed savagely. There was also an onslaught on our society's drapery department in Caroline Street, but the mob desisted when it was found that the shop was not Mr. Ashton's property. Two adjoining shops were used as relief stores. They were quickly broken open, and a scene more disgraceful perhaps than any other enacted. Piles of clothing and cloth were hurled out of the upper windows to the people in the street.

A cry was raised that the soldiers were coming, but amidst laughter from the mob it was declared to be only a woman in a red cloak, and the work of destruction went on, several things being wantonly set on fire, until, a little after half-past five, a company of the 14th Hussars from the Ashton Barracks, under the command of Captain Chapman, appeared in sight. The soldiers galloped along flourishing their swords, and every one in the crowd looked to his or her personal safety. Some of those still in the store, in attempting a hasty retreat, fell at the entrance; others behind were thrown upon them, and there the people lay, five or six deep, male and female, when the soldiers reached them. The police were almost as soon as the Hussars, and some who had created such havoc were easily captured. Amidst the hooting and yelling, Mr. D. Harrison read the Riot Act, and the troops proceeded to clear the streets. To escape detection some of the plunderers burned the clothing; others threw it into the canal and the river Tame, and various articles of wearing apparel could be seen for some time floating on the water. Special constables were sworn in, armed with sabres, and arrangements were made for the calling in of fifty of the Cheshire police force should their services be required. Under the protection of the military the police visited certain parts of the town, where they found large quantities of the stolen clothing, and many more people were taken into custody. At 10 o'clock the soldiers were called off and the town was left to the guardianship of the police and special constables. When the prisoners were brought before the magistrates they were admonished by Mr. David Harrison (chairman) and Mr. John Cheetham. It was a most disgraceful thing, they were told, that after so much had been done for the people the benefactors should be turned upon and abused as they had been. Mr. Bates, for instance, had opened his door to the people, and this was the return they had made for his kindness. He (Mr. Cheetham) had been speaking publicly in London, within a fortnight, of the high character he thought they had won for their patience and forbearance under their trials. He felt it deeply; he felt that they had not only alienated the people at a distance, but had disgraced the town. Many of the prisoners were committed to Chester for riot.

There was further resistance to the police and military when two omnibuses appeared for the purpose of conveying the prisoners to the railway station to take train for Chester, brickbats and other missiles being thrown. The people vowed that they would have something to eat before they went to bed, and would " clem " no longer. Prisoners to the number of 29 were placed in a separate railway carriage and left the station amidst loud cheering. Twice the cavalry rode through the mob, creating the greatest consternation, and a company of infantry marched the streets with fixed bayonets, but little personal injury was done. On one or two occasions blood was drawn; the sight of it had a great effect on the crowd, and order was restored.

In the spring and summer of 1865 a few more hands were employed in the mills. When the panic was at its height there were, it is said, 730 houses and shops empty, and in October, 1866, there were still 620. It was estimated that before the panic had lasted two years about 1,000 persons had emigrated, and from 1861 to 1866 the population had decreased by 2,000. At the height of the distress there was the extraordinary spectacle of 84 persons emigrating to Australia in a body, headed through the town by a band of music, with flags flying and thousands of people cheering.

Mr. William Cooper, referred to elsewhere as the first cashier of the Rochdale Pioneers, wrote to Mr. Holyoake that Stalybridge, Ashton, Mossley, Duk'nfield, Hyde, Heywood, Middleton, and Rawtenstall had suffered badly, being almost entirely cotton manufacturing towns, but that none of the stores had failed, so that, taken altogether, the co-operative societies in Lancashire were as numerous and as strong after the cotton panic as before it set in. Mr. Cooper wrote of Manchester at the same time rather contemptuously, that it was good for nothing then except to sell cotton. But even Manchester, he said, had created a Manchester and Salford store, maintained for five years an average of 1,200 members, and made for them £7,000 of profit. What would Mr. Cooper think now, we wonder, of the same Manchester and Salford store, with its 18,000 members?

In 1852 Mr. T. Bazley warned the country of the danger of trusting to America alone for cotton. In 1857 there was formed the Cotton Supply Association, with our townsman, the late John Cheetham, M.P., as president. The scheme had its inception in the fears of a portion of the trade that some dire calamity must sooner or later overtake the cotton manufacture of Lancashire if it were left to depend upon the treacherous foundation of slave-labour as the main source of its raw material. The association established agencies in various countries, and distributed large consignments of cotton seed and preparatory machinery, but the scheme did not meet with the support it deserved.

In May, 1862, Mr. Bazley stated that through the failure of the American supply the loss to the labouring classes was £12,000,000 a year, and estimated the loss including the employing classes at nearly £40,000,000 a year. In the Lancashire district—population about 4,000,000—there were receiving parish relief, September,

1861, 43,500 persons; in September, 1862, 163,498. The Union Relief Act, passed August, 1862, gave much relief by enabling overseers to borrow money to be expended in public works executed by the unemployed workmen. In October, 1864, much distress still existed, and fears for the approaching winter were entertained. At that time, it was stated in the *Times* of 18th January, 1865, there were 90,000 more paupers than ordinary in cotton districts. In June, 1865, a special commissioner appointed in May, 1862, was recalled by the Poor Law Board, and the famine was declared ended. £1,000,000 had been expended in two years. The executive of the central relief fund held their last meeting on the 4th December, 1865.

PART II.

CHAPTER I.

THE START AT STALYBRIDGE.
F.R.S. and LL.D.
Can only spring from A B C.
—*Eliza Cook*.

WHAT is described in the society's records as the preliminary meeting was held on the 7th March, 1859, but Mr. Charles Wright, of Manchester and Salford Society, carries us back six days to the first of that month. He points out that the *Co-operator*, a monthly journal of the period, of August, 1860, gives an account of a meeting on the earlier date. Eleven persons were present, and they met " to discuss the practicability of opening a store where the working man's wife might purchase with safety and advantage those articles of consumption which are daily required in the homes of working men." A copy of the rules of the Rochdale Pioneers was sent for and adapted to local circumstances.

On the first meeting night twenty-two £1 shares were taken up. No names are given, and there is some uncertainty as to the identity of those present ;

48   CO-OPERATION IN STALYBRIDGE.

but what appears to be the first share ledger has been traced, and it shows that the numbers 1 to 22 were allotted as follows :—

1 Alexander Maxwell
2 Ambrose Jackson
3 Dan Woolley
4 John Peacock
5 Thomas Baxter
6 Thomas Phillips
7 Charles Gaskill
8 William Haynes
9 Henry Pool
10 Joseph Edgar
11 Johanan Booth
12 Henry Bradley
13 John Shaw
14 Jonathan Blacker
15 Charles Rodgers
16 Jerry Ratcliffe
17 Joseph Woolhouse
18 John Dearnaley
19 John France
20 Devenport Davis
21 John Holding
22 Hiram Ratcliffe

Following these, there were admitted as members :—

23 John Bradbury
24 William Harrison
25 Thomas Ellis
26 Thomas Hornby
27 Thomas Lockwood
28 James Heywood
29 Joshua Allsop
30 John Langford Porter
31 Daniel Marsland
32 Joseph Bailey
33 Abel Frederick Wood
34 John Hassall
35 Martha Norminton
36 John Holt
37 Robert Winterbottom
38 Mary Moss
39 Joseph Allen, jun.
40 William Greenwood
41 Joshua Hill
42 James Cook
43 William Howarth
44 John Cheetham
45 George Woodhead
46 William Simpson
47 Benjamin Hurst
48 Henry Sheppard
49 Joseph Swift
50 Arnold Rowbottom
51 John Whiteley
52 John Beswick
53 John Cocker
54 James Haughton
55 Charles Haughton
56 John Miller
57 Nancy Hassall
58 Joseph Allen, sen.
59 Charles Marsland
60 George France
61 John Duffy
62 Charles Jones
63 Edward Booth
64 William Campbell
65 James Kenworthy
66 William Brougham
67 Giles Hinchcliffe
68 Samuel Platt

CO-OPERATION IN STALYBRIDGE. 49

69	Thomas Jones	86	Joseph Roebuck
70	John Ridgway	87	John Marsden
71	Thomas Lee	88	Henry Clayton
72	Joshua Andrew	89	Samuel Lowe
73	Joseph Hill	90	Abraham Lawton
74	William Banton	91	Bradburn Cocker
75	George Kay	92	Ratcliffe Buckley
76	John Smith	93	James Cooper
77	William Lowe	94	George Barker
78	James Kay	95	Henry Langley
79	Hugh Kenworthy	96	John Jones
80	John Thorp	97	David Hastings
81	Joseph McQuire	98	Charles Deakin
82	George Kiddy	99	Thomas Haslam
83	William Haynes, sen.	100	Josiah Rigby
84	John Eastwood	101	James Mitchell
85	James Lee	102	Samuel Sykes

There were some alterations of the machine paging of the ledger in which these names appear, hence there is some uncertainty as to the numbers; but all the names appear in the order and under the numbers given, and all are those of members admitted during 1859 and 1860. They are detailed here because they appear to be what may be called original members, that is, first holders of the share accounts so numbered.

One of the early share accounts had been closed and balanced, apparently for withdrawal, and either the member had changed his mind or it was found that the entries were intended for another account. For some reason the ledger folio bears the remark, " account closed wrongfully," and shows that the account was reopened, an instance of the strong language inadvertently used by some people. Clearly, the book-keeper who wrote the remark meant, not that a wrong had been done, but that there had been a slight error.

The first minute book is still in existence, and it is recorded that the following resolutions were carried at the meeting held 7th March, 1859 :—

1. That the shares be £1 each, and that the subscription be 1s. per week.
2. That no member have less than one share, nor more than five shares.
3. That Johanan Booth be treasurer and Thomas Baxter secretary for the time being.
4. That the contributions be brought to the house of James Cook every Monday fortnight, betwixt the hours of seven and nine of the clock.
5. That every member who is six weeks in arrear be fined threepence, and if three months in arrear be excluded, except sufficient cause be shown to the committee why they or he should not.
6. That the following members form the committee :—Charles Gaskill, Daniel Woolley, Ambrose Jackson, William Haynes, Alexander Maxwell, Joseph Edgar.
7. That 1,000 handbills be printed, and that A. Maxwell and Thomas Phillips see that they be printed.
8. That the committee meet on Wednesday night, March 9th, for the purpose of drawing up a handbill for delivery among the public.

(Signed) THOMAS BAXTER, Secretary.

JOHANAN BOOTH, Chairman.

CO-OPERATION IN STALYBRIDGE. 51

There were also present at this meeting Henry Pool and John Peacock. Thus, assuming that the others named in the resolutions—six forming the committee, and Messrs. Booth, Baxter, Cook, and Phillips—were all present, there would be a total attendance of twelve persons.

Other members admitted during 1859 were :—

John Bamford	Michael O'Donnel.
Richard Bentinck	Frederick Brown
George Rainforth	Betty Dearnaley
Joseph Sykes	Edward Davis
Henry Dyson	Augustus Ball
John Crossley	James Hill
James Hallam	Ann Chadwick
George Rushton	John Lyttle
Henry Hurst	Ben Platt
William Wood	James Lomas
Harriet Sykes	Randal Cheetham

Mr. James Bamford, of Huddersfield Road, became a member in 1859, before the society was registered. The writer learned from him that the movement originated at Messrs. Harrison's mill. Mr. Bamford says the mill and a beerhouse in Harrop Street joined ; the latter was the house of James Cook, referred to in the fourth resolution of the March 7th meeting.

Mr. Baxter's inquiry for a form of declaration brought forth from the Rochdale Equitable Pioneers' Co-operative Society a reply addressed from Nos. 8, 16, and 31, Toad Lane, March 12th, 1859, offering to get made a declaration and proposition book, arranged to conform to the Stalybridge rules. Our Rochdale friends had paper printed and partly ruled ready for the making up of such a book. They had also a wholesale department for supplying goods to other societies. In a letter dated May 25th they expressed pleasure at the progress-making at Stalybridge, and thought business might be commenced in a small way before November or December. Many of the letters at this time were addressed to Mr. Baxter, 30, Wakefield Road, Stalybridge.

At the meeting held March 9th, 1859, the secretary was instructed to write to Rochdale for a form of declaration to make members, and was empowered to buy the books that were necessary to record the minutes and to keep the accounts. The entrance fee was fixed at one shilling per share.

The first general meeting was held March 21st, 1859. John Bradbury, John France, and Johanan Booth were elected trustees, and William Haynes and Joseph Woolhouse money stewards. At the same meeting it was resolved that any officer being absent after 7 o'clock on any meeting night be fined threepence, to go to the incidental expenses fund.

At a meeting held April 4th, 1859, a committee composed of John France, Charles Rodgers, Thomas Ellis, Jonathan Blacker, Thomas Hornby, and James Heywood was formed to revise the rules. Three days later the contribution was reduced from a shilling to sixpence per week, and it was decided that dividend on purchases should be paid to non-members. On the 21st April it was resolved that a member be allowed ten shares instead of five, and on the 9th May this was further extended to twenty shares. At the same meeting Johanan Booth was authorised to take up five shares of the Rochdale Corn Mill Society, and the rules passed by John Tidd Pratt, Esq., Registrar of

Friendly Societies, were adopted. The Registrar's certificate reads—

"I hereby certify that these rules are in conformity to law and to the provisions of the Statute 15 and 16, Vict. c. 31, relating to Industrial and Provident Societies.

"JOHN TIDD PRATT,
"The Registrar of Friendly Societies
"Copy kept,   in England.
"J. Tidd Pratt.   "9th June, 1859."

Premises in Water Street, then in the occupation of Mr. Joshua Crowther, were taken on the 16th May, 1859, and in September Messrs. France and Edgar were appointed to go to Mr. Crowther to bargain for whatever he might have to dispose of that would suit the purposes of the society. It was decided that the words " Stalybridge Co-operative Stores, enrolled under Act of Parliament," should be painted on the sign.

The first record of the election of officers after the society was established in Water Street is dated 23rd June, 1859. Thomas Baxter was appointed secretary for twelve months, and the following gentlemen were elected to other offices for the same period :—

Committee—Joseph Edgar, Thomas Ellis, Charles Gaskill, Joseph Woolhouse, Daniel Woolley, James Heywood, Jonathan Blacker, Joseph Allen, and John Langford Porter.

Auditors—Alexander Maxwell and Joshua Allsop.

Trustees—John France, Abel Frederick Wood, and James Cook.

Treasurer—Johanan Booth.

Money Stewards—Robert Winterbottom and Joseph Bailey.

At this meeting there were also appointed five Arbitrators :—Matthew Hutchinson, Tom Milburn, Frank Farrow, Robert Whitehead, and Nathan Pickering.

The first reference to remuneration of an officer is under the date November 17th, 1859, when the secretary's salary was fixed at twenty-eight shillings per quarter as from November 1st. Some months later the treasurer's salary was fixed at £5 per annum, and the persons who took stock were to have sixpence each for their trouble.

In June and July, 1859, there were resolutions admitting " as fit and proper persons to be members of this society," Benjamin Hurst, Henry Sheppard, Joseph Swift, William Simpson, George Woodhead, Arnold Rowbottom, John Whiteley, and John Beswick.

It is probable that about this time useful information was obtained from Rochdale and other towns. Johanan Booth was requested to " make a bill of his expenses to and from Rochdale," and it was resolved that all the books of account be purchased from William Cooper, who was the first cashier appointed by the Rochdale Pioneers.

James Heywood was appointed to go to Rochdale to glean whatever information he could from the storekeeper there, Charles Gaskill and Joseph Woolhouse to go to Dukinfield and Mossley to get information respecting their mode of conducting business, and Johanan Booth was appointed to represent the society at Mossley Society's tea party, which was held on Saturday, February 18th, 1860.

Our pioneers were evidently for a time dependent for fixtures and utensils in trade on the former tenant of the shop, for it was resolved—"That we put ourselves in a state of independence as regards shop fixtures, and that Joseph Edgar and Johanan Booth are engaged by this committee (with power to add to their number) to make all the shop fixtures that are required. That we have baywood tops to the counters." About the same time Messrs. Heywood, Gaskill, and Ellis were deputed to go to Manchester to purchase scales, weights, canisters, &c., and they were to take a few pounds with them to be left on articles as deposits. Later, Frank Farrow was sent to convey the scales, &c., to Stalybridge, and he was to take the money to pay for them. A vote of thanks to Mr. Ellis was passed "for his exertions on behalf of this society at Manchester in getting discount off the articles bought at Sutcliffe's, canister manufacturer."

On the 12th September, 1859, it was decided to advertise in the *Ashton Reporter*, *Ashton Standard*, and a Rochdale paper for a shopman, and that the security to be given by the shopman should be "£100 or two fifties." On the 22nd that portion of the resolution referring to insertion in a Rochdale paper was rescinded. The committee met October 11th to select a shopman from the applicants, and James Hyde was appointed at "26s. per week and sleeping room." It was arranged that he should commence his duties on the 31st October, and the trustees were asked to look to the shopman for his security. The "£100 or two fifties" was not forthcoming, and it was decided that the matter be referred to a guarantee society, the premium to be paid by the employers until the wages of the employed had been reconsidered. This reconsideration took place in January, 1860, and the remuneration was increased to thirty shillings per week and four shillings for expenses. Mr. Hyde and Mr. Baxter, the secretary, were to go together "to buy good groceries for and on behalf of this society," and William Leech was offered a situation as assistant at twelve shillings per week for a month. It appears that Mr. Hyde lent money to the society, for in January, 1860, there was a resolution authorising payment to him of £1 for interest on money used for the society's purposes during the previous quarter. It is evident, too, that Mr. Hyde gave good service, and that the committee appreciated. On the 9th February, 1860, there was a resolution—"That James Hyde have a vote of thanks from this meeting for the efficient manner in which he has discharged the duties of his situation during the past quarter."

In October, 1859, there was passed a resolution that the treasurer for the time being be allowed to sit on the committee and to vote on any question under discussion. At the same meeting it was resolved "that we have checks"—the first reference to the method of keeping account of members' purchases— and the quantities of checks to be bought were 4,000 pence checks, 2,000 shilling checks, and 1,000 copper checks, with a set of figures. About the same time it was decided that any person buying wholesale at the store, whether a member or not, should not have checks.

A minute penned on the 27th October, 1859, is somewhat problematic. It was resolved—"That we keep the first quarter's dividend among ourselves." At first thought, this savours of a summary method of distributing the profits, but it may be that the resolution indicates merely a determination not to disclose details to outsiders by publication. During the same month the secretary was instructed to write to Joseph Clarkson, tea dealer, Huddersfield, requesting him to send his representative with samples.

It appears that during the very month in which the Stalybridge Society commenced business—indeed, a few days before the shop was opened—amalgamation with the Dukinfield Society was suggested. It was decided on the 2nd November, 1859, that the matter be laid before the general meeting, and a vote of thanks to the Dukinfield Committee was passed ; but, so far as the writer can gather, there was no development of the scheme.

The first report of the committee has not been traced, but the second, pen-written, is in existence and is as follows :—

STALYBRIDGE CO-OPERATIVE SOCIETY.

THE SECOND QUARTERLY REPORT OF THE SOCIETY'S ACCOUNTS FOR THE QUARTER ENDING OCTOBER 4TH, 1859.

RECEIPTS.	£	s.	d.	DISBURSEMENTS.	£	s.	d.
To Cash Balance, July Quarter	44	12	6	Printing 60 Bills	0	7	6
Propositions	3	7	2	For Posting the above	0	2	6
Contributions	162	5	6	Stationery and Stamps	0	3	5½
Discount of Bills	0	7	1½	Account Books	4	4	6
Sold one Book of Rules	0	0	4	Mr. Booth's Expenses to Rochdale	0	8	0
Sold two Sheets of Paper	0	0	0½	Three Men's Expenses to Manchester to purchase articles	0	13	6
				Canisters, Coffee Mill, Twine Box, Show Bowls, Snuff Box, Truck, Coffee Box and Sieve	12	7	6
				Scales, Weights, and Weighing Machine	13	8	6
				Timber for Counter and other Joiners' work	7	0	10½
				Carriage of the above	0	9	9
				Withdrawn	0	1	11
				Advertisement for Shopman	0	1	9
				Joshua Crowther, for Shop Fittings and Rent	3	3	9
				Banking Book	0	0	3
				Total Expenditure	42	13	9
				Balance in hand	167	18	11
	£210	12	8		£210	12	8

CO-OPERATION IN STALYBRIDGE.

	£	s.	d.
Cash in hand	167	18	11
Invested in Rochdale District Corn Mill Society	5	0	0
Society's Worth in Cash	172	18	11
Society's Worth in Goods	25	17	0
Worth in Cash and Goods	£198	15	11

JOSHUA ALLSOP,
ALEXANDER MAXWELL, } *Auditors.*

Even at this early stage the committee had such confidence that they decided on the 10th November, 1859, to take the shop on a lease for fourteen years. There were some willing helpers at shop-fitting and in other directions. There was a vote of thanks to Mr. John Miller for the valuable services he had rendered the society in lending men and tools, and another to the joiners for the complete manner in which they had fitted up the shop and for their usefulness generally. A few months later one member, who had £5. 0s. 9d. to his credit, found it necessary for some reason to withdraw. He withdrew the pounds; the share ledger bears the remark opposite the balance of ninepence—" Presented to reading room." Every little helps, and doubtless the spirit that prompted the presentation of that ninepence was appreciated.

CHAPTER II.

THE OPENING IN WATER STREET.

Think naught a trifle, though it small appear ;
Small sands the mountain ; moments make the year ;
And trifles life.
—*Young.*

BUSINESS in Water Street was commenced on the 11th November, 1859. The writer's father remembers, as a tradesman, how the shopkeepers received the news. They said : " They're startin' a co-op. ; we me't as well shut up." There was a capital of £210, held by 139 members. The opening proved a great success, for at the close of the first week £84. 10s. 2½d. had been taken over the counter. Thomas Ellis was deputed to go to Richard Bentinck to get information respecting insurance premiums, and in December it was decided that the stock of groceries be insured in the Sun Fire Office for £500.

From insurance the deliberations passed to pork, and it was resolved—" That Johanan Booth buy Edward Stanley's pig for this society." At another meeting it was decided that no New Year gifts be granted to members or others. At this time there were to be printed 2,000 copies of a notice and two dozen notice cards, the cards to announce that members must bring in their rule books and checks not later than the following Saturday, and Samuel Harrison was to have the preference for the printer's work if he could complete it in time.

At this early period, too, butchering was essayed, and a sub-committee formed to look out a site or a building for a butcher's shop and slaughter-house. The result of the inquiry was that there was taken a shop " at the top end of Caroline Street " for the sale of butcher's meat, and a slaughter-house belonging to the Foresters' Society in Vaudrey Street. The butchering utensils of Henry Dyson and George Kay were bought, and Arnold Kay was appointed butcher to the society on the 3rd April, 1860, at a weekly wage, together with house and gas free. The gas-fitting in the shop was to be done by James Smith, if he could do it in time. At the same time the making of a handcart was placed in the hands of Frank Longden, and the painting and sign-writing was entrusted to Oliver N. Gatley, who was in business in Grosvenor Street where the Central premises are now situated.

At this time a dividend of 9d. per £ was declared, and it was decided that the report should be printed. Three hundred copies were to be obtained, and the printer's work was done by H. and S. Burgess, of Stalybridge and Ashton. During the same year other printers' work was placed in the hands of Mrs. Cunningham. There was an effort to find work for the members, a resolution being passed—" That the carriage of goods for the store be divided amongst the members alone, as far as possible."

From the day of opening in Water Street to the end of the quarter—the society's third quarter, but the first open for the sale of goods—members increased daily, and the total sales were £1,132. 18s. 3d. It appears, however, that consumers were not entitled to dividend on the whole of this, as a dividend at the rate of 9d. per £ was declared on £300 only. The profit on some articles was precarious. On sugar, for instance, no dividend was paid. The report and accounts were as follows :—

THE STALYBRIDGE INDUSTRIAL CO-OPERATIVE SOCIETY.

The Third Quarterly Report of the Accounts of the Society for the Quarter Ending January 31st, 1860.

Your committee feel great pleasure in issuing this their third quarterly report, showing the progress that has been made during the last quarter, and taking into consideration the difficulties that we have had to contend with feel assured that our efforts have not been in vain; the committee wish to impress upon all the members the necessity as far as practicable of dealing at the Society's store, being convinced that it is the only true source from whence profit will accrue to the members.

Your committee has great pleasure in being able to give ninepence in the pound on members' purchases this quarter, the first quarter that the Society's Store has been open, and hope and trust that the spirit of co-operation will cause each and all of the members to have that zeal and confidence in the society which cannot fail to have good results.

CASH ACCOUNT.

RECEIPTS.	£	s.	d.	DISBURSEMENTS.	£	s.	d.
Balance in hand last quarter	167	18	11	Cash paid Goods, Groceries, &c.	1413	15	8½
Received for Goods, Groceries, &c.	1132	18	3½	Carriage	11	12	11
Discount at Bills	23	16	7	License	0	12	7
Contributions	614	1	7	Fixed Stock Additions	83	17	0
Propositions	7	4	1	Wages	29	2	9
Nominations	0	7	6	Printing and Stationery	2	18	2
Empty Sacks returned	5	0	0	Guarantee Premium	2	7	6
Bank Interest	0	15	9	Fire Assurance	1	2	6
				Coals	0	13	7
				Gas	2	12	2
				Withdrawals	3	6	0
				Cash in hand	400	1	10
	£1952	2	8½		£1952	2	8½

GENERAL STATEMENT.

LIABILITIES.	£	s.	d.
Members' Claims, as per Ledger	823	4	2
One Quarter's Rent	4	0	0
Interest on Paid-up Shares	4	0	0
Reserve Fund	8	6	8
Balance Profit	11	5	0
	£850	15	10

ASSETS.	£	s.	d.
Fixed Stock Account	29	11	0
Fixed Stock Additions	83	17	0
Invested in the Rochdale District Corn Mill	5	0	0
Interest added to our account therein	5	6	0
Goods in Stock	327	0	0
Cash in hand	400	1	10
	£850	15	10

PROFIT ACCOUNT.

	£	s.	d.
Dividend on £300 purchase money at 9d. in the pound	11	5	0
	£11	5	0

	£	s.	d.
Balance Profit	11	5	0
	£11	5	0

JOSHUA ALLSOP,
ALEXANDER MAXWELL, } Auditors.

Some of the early resolutions go into detail, and in others quaint expressions are used. One on the 6th March, 1860, reads—" That the shelves required in the shop be put up, and that a saw be bought for the use of the shopman to saw bones." Another on the same date is—" Moved by Charles Gaskill, seconded by Cook James *vice versa*, that the Act of Parliament relating to Friendly and Provident Societies be bought." Another resolution appointed two members of the committee to go to the Temperance Room to look at some forms on sale there, and if they thought the articles worth the price, they were to buy them. Still another reads—" That there be two books provided for the store, one to be called the petty cash book and the other to be called the inventory book, to put all the articles in that belong to the society;" and another—" That any member can have his money at sight if there is cash in hand that will pay him, unless the money be wanted for some uses of the society more urgent." Not all the resolutions are so explicit, however. One reads—" That one thousand summonses be obtained," but it is not stated whether they were summonses to a meeting or to a Court, nor on whom they were to be served.

A sub-committee was appointed to look out a room for the society to hold its meetings in, and on the 12th April, 1860, the Foresters' Hall, in Vaudrey Street, was taken for the purpose. About the same time there was taken a room in the Angel Inn yard, belonging to James Wilson, at the yearly rent of five guineas. A dozen forms were to be made, and Joseph Edgar was to buy the table of John Marshall for the room.

Mr. W. Evans (once a member of the Stalybridge Town Council), who became a member of the society about October, 1859, remembers that the room was used as the society's office, whilst the Water Street shop was still used for sales. He has a lively recollection of the long queue waiting to pay share contributions and take up their books. Mr. Evans' first share book is still in his possession.

In April, 1860, a sub-committee was appointed to inquire about the shop of Butterworth's in Caroline Street, with a view to taking it, if suitable, for drapery. On the 17th April, John Marshall was appointed to fit up for drapery the shop No. 58, Caroline Street, and William Lowe was engaged to clean it. An advertisement was inserted in the Manchester *Guardian* on the two following Saturdays, April 21st and 28th, for a "shopman draper;" he was to be a married man and give security in £100. The remuneration was fixed at 26s. per week for the draper himself and 8s. per week for his wife. Four of the applicants were invited to meet the committee, their references were investigated, and on the 8th May James Frederick Keeley was appointed, to commence his duties on Monday, the 14th May, 1860. The committee restricted him in his buying to three wholesale houses, those of Messrs. S. and J. Watts, Messrs. Thorp and Son, and Messrs. J. and N. Philips. The stock and fixtures were shortly afterwards insured for £500 with the Sun Fire Office. Mr. Keeley was not long employed. On the 19th July, 1860, a Mr. Edwards was appointed draper, but the resolution was rescinded at the next meeting, and it was left to Mr. Hyde, who was appointed general manager at the same meeting, July 26th, to inquire for a draper. At this point there is a gap in the records. The minutes from 1860 to 1865 are missing. It is known, however, that Miss Hampshire was employed in drapery in Caroline Street, and was still in the department when it was removed to Grosvenor Street; she followed Mrs. Rowbotham, wife of Mr. Henry Rowbotham, who was manager after Mr. Hyde left.

A general meeting for the election of officers was held in the Foresters' Hall, Vaudrey Street, on the 1st May, 1860, and the following were elected :—

> Committee—Thomas Ellis, Charles Gaskill, Daniel Woolley, Joseph Edgar, Joseph Allen, Joseph Woolhouse, George Kay, Alexander Maxwell, and James Heywood.
>
> Trustees—John France, James Cook, and Robert Marsland.
>
> Stewards—Joseph Bailey and Robert Winterbottom.
>
> Auditors—Joshua Allsop and Bradburn Cocker.
>
> Treasurer—Johanan Booth.
>
> Secretary—Thomas Baxter.
>
> Arbitrators—Matthew Hutchinson, Tom Milburn, Nathan Pickering, Robert Whitehead, and Frank Farrow.

At this time the committee felt justified in employing the secretary whole time, and on the 10th May, 1860, the resolution passed on 17th November fixing the secretary's remuneration at 28s. per quarter was rescinded, and he was appointed at £1 per week to undertake the duties of secretary and to make himself generally useful. He was asked to seek the advice of Mr. Occleshaw who was manager of the Stalybridge Branch of the Manchester and Liverpool District Banking Company Limited, and on the 17th May it was decided to open an account with the District Bank. A week later the trustees were requested to go to Mr. Noah Buckley, attorney, to have prepared an indenture between the society and Albert Newton, butcher's assistant, and on the 31st May it was arranged that the trustees should go to Mr. Wilson, Butterworth's agent, on the 12th June, " to see all things settled and right as regards the drapers' store and the stable behind for a slaughter-house."

In June the same year it was resolved that one share be taken up in *The Co-operator* newspaper, published by the Literary Committee of the Co-operative Society, Great Ancoats Street, Manchester. It is evident that the committee's attention to detail was great, for there was a resolution penned the same month that there be a slate bought for the use of the secretary, and another that a large ledger be bought for the purpose of keeping account of members' investments. There is here what appears to be the first reference to the occupation of Grosvenor Street premises, Mr. Hyde being instructed to find a man for the branch store there.

At the end of the fourth quarter there were 480 members, and the number of shares taken up was 1,500, 1,300 of which were fully paid. The committee reported as follows :—

> We have now in connection with our store a butcher's shop, which kills weekly an ox, six sheep, one calf, one lamb, and occasionally a pig ; which, considering the high price of flesh meat, we think pretty good. We have also

opened a shop for drapery, which took for goods sold £34. 10s. the first week, and promises to do well ; for our wives and children are always wanting frocks, bonnets, &c., and I suppose we men-folks require shirts, &c.

We may just mention that, through the jealousy and interference of the shopkeepers, and the fear of the landlords, we were nearly two months before we could get anyone to let us a shop ; but these drawbacks only stimulated us the more when we got one, and we are now reaping the reward of our labour, for we forgot to mention that our dividend was 1s. 3d. in the pound, and last week we took in the grocery shop alone £203. 0s. 3d., to say nothing of the butchery and drapery.

We are all working men ; our treasurer is a joiner, and the secretary a blacksmith, though we have decided to take the latter away from the anvil, and put him to the business of our society.

Our committee have decided to take up shares in the company for conducting your (or we would rather say our) journal ; for we think it is a first-rate affair, and just the paper that ought to be placed in the hands of every working man. We may say, in conclusion, that we intend very shortly inaugurating a newsroom and library, where our members can, free of charge, read and converse, and where solid instruction can be obtained.

Mr. Charles Wright says, referring to this report, that it is very interesting to find that education was not lost sight of by our pioneers, and that they believed intelligence was a paying investment.

CHAPTER III.

THE FIRST TEA PARTY.

AT the end of June, 1860, there was held in the large room of the Foresters' Hall a tea party, the proceeds of which were to be devoted to the formation of the newsroom and library just referred to. Upwards of 600 persons sat down to tea, which was amply provided by members of the society. A brass band was in attendance, and the audience was delighted during the evening by select pieces of music at intervals. After the tables had been cleared, the Mayor, Thomas Hadfield Sidebottom, Esq., took the chair amidst enthusiastic applause, and accompanying him on the platform were Moses Hadfield, Esq., J.P.; Mr. Abraham Greenwood, of the Rochdale Pioneers' Society; Mr. Edward Longfield, president of the Manchester and Salford Equitable Co-operative Society; and Mr. William Marcroft, one of the founders of the Oldham Industrial Society. It was at Mr. Marcroft's that the first officially recorded meeting of that society was held.

72 CO-OPERATION IN STALYBRIDGE.

The Chairman, in opening the proceedings, said he took the chair with very great pleasure. They were all aware of the object for which they had met, and therefore it would be unnecessary for him to go into it. But, with reference to the co-operative societies in Manchester, Rochdale, and other places, he could say that they had attained very great success. The formation of a library and newsroom in connection with the Stalybridge Co-operative Society was a noble achievement, and he could assure the audience that he wished the society every success and prosperity. That was their first meeting, and he hoped it would not be the last; it was very well attended, and he hoped the next would be doubly so, and that their gatherings would keep on doubling. There was nothing more beneficial than to be members of a good library.

Mr. Hadfield then addressed the meeting. He was glad, he said, to see the Mayor occupying the chair on that occasion. He could not be better engaged in his official capacity, nor in a more worthy cause, for that, in his opinion, was an active endeavour on the part of the people to improve their condition, and he must congratulate the meeting on the numerous assembly that evening. It augured well for the success of the society. The history of the workers hitherto had been of a varied character, and they had been subject to many evils; but as society was progressing in the arts and sciences, the workers apparently were not behind the times. That there was progress among them there could be no doubt, because he believed the Stalybridge Co-operative Society was composed of the most intelligent, the most industrious, and the most careful

CO-OPERATION IN STALYBRIDGE. 73

of the workers of Stalybridge. There must be progress so long as this was the case, and it struck him that they must be successful in their endeavours. That society had only been in existence about eight months, and it was doing a fair and favourable business, taking, he believed, about £101 per day. The society had opened a butcher's and a draper's shop, and each was doing a good business. But perhaps they owed their rapid progress in Stalybridge in a great measure to the noble and trustworthy individuals in Rochdale, who appeared to be the pioneers of the movement. The people of Rochdale had gone through a great deal of up-hill work; they had proved the worth and practicability of co-operation; and he thought too much praise could not be given them. Mr. John Bright had made the following statement in the House of Commons a short time before :—" The Rochdale Pioneers' Society was established in 1844, with 28 members and a capital of £28; at the end of 1859 it had 2,703 members and a capital of £27,060. It had done a business during the year of £104,000, and had divided amongst its members a sum of £10,739. Two-and-a-half per cent of the profits, amounting in the past year to £300, was deducted for the purchase of books, newspapers, &c., for the use of the members' reading-room. The library contained about 4,000 volumes, and was increasing rapidly every quarter. There was likewise a Sabbath School attached to the institution. The working men of Rochdale established a corn mill in 1850. In 1851 the capital was £2,163, and in that year it suffered a loss of £421, which sum was made up by subsequent profits before any division was made. At the end of 1859 the capital of the corn Mill Society was £18,236, the business done £85,845, and the profit £6,115. A co-operative manufacturing society had been established in Rochdale, consisting of 1,600 members with a capital of £50,000." Now, considering the success which had attended the labours of the Rochdale Pioneers, he (Mr. Hadfield) did not see anything to prevent the Stalybridge Society going on in a similar manner. The town was favourably situated, and the people received as good wages as in any other part of England; therefore, in the hands of the energetic and hard working people whom he saw before him, he thought the progress of the Stalybridge Society might be even more rapid than that of the Rochdale Pioneers. It was a little over twelve months since the first eleven Stalybridge co-operators met and established that society, and they had continued to meet fortnightly up to that time, and with considerable success. On the 11th November, 1859, the first store for the sale of groceries was opened. At that time they had 139 members, with a capital of £210. Since then the society's progress had been so rapid that it had never been surpassed, and never, he believed, equalled. The receipts the first week the store was open were £84. This had increased in thirteen weeks to £119 for the week, and they were enabled to give 9d. in the £ dividend, with 5 per cent interest on paid-up capital. At the commencement of the following quarter the number of members had increased to 247, with a capital of £420, whilst the weekly sales ranged from £118 to £160. About that time great difficulty was experienced in obtaining a shop for butchering,

CO-OPERATION IN STALYBRIDGE. 75

and great credit was due to the sub-committee and a few of the members who nobly seconded their endeavours. They had now a butcher's shop where there were sold beef and mutton of a quality not often met with in that neighbourhood. At the commencement of the present quarter the number of members was 377, with a capital of £1,219, and that was increasing rapidly, for, although only two months were passed, the number of members was 575 and the capital £2,000. The weekly sales in grocery alone were £250, and with butchering and drapery added, the amount drawn over the counter at the present time was £314; a grocer, with one assistant and a man to weigh flour, actually taking £101 in one day. With such an accumulation of funds they were obliged to open another store, and a shop was taken for the drapery business. The shop was stocked with an excellent assortment of goods, and it was to be hoped that all co-operators would trade there for any draperies they might require. (Hear, hear.) Something had been said about the formation of a library and reading-room. That was a matter which must be attended to after man had been supplied with food and raiment, and the common necessaries of life.

Mr. Abraham Greenwood said the Stalybridge Society had made an excellent beginning, and he did not see why they should not do as they had done at Rochdale. There the members had great advantages. They had their food pure and unadulterated, as far as it could be procured; at all events, they got their goods from the manufacturers and large dealers, and did not allow any intermediate dealers, where it could be prevented, to interfere between those who manufactured and those who consumed the commodities. Another advantage to be derived from co-operation was that it made people better friends. To those who differed in politics and religion it was neutral ground on which they could meet and have friendly intercourse ; it created a better feeling and confidence than had hitherto been attainable. The Rochdale Society had men of all religious opinions and shades of politics, and they all agreed to persevere for each others' interest. They had a capital of £32,513 ; they had done a business during the past quarter of £35,561, had paid in wages about £900, and had realised profits at the store alone at the rate of over £15,000 a year. They had about eighty-six men engaged in the different departments, including six in drapery, three clerks, eight butchers, seventeen boot and shoe makers, ten cloggers, and ten tailors, with one general manager. He was glad to see the Stalybridge people making an effort to raise an educational fund. He conceived that nothing had done them more credit at Rochdale than that part of their co-operation ; and he thought they had created for themselves advantages in that way which were never put within the reach of working men before. The amount they devoted to education was $2\frac{1}{2}$ per cent of the net profits, and the remainder was divided in the usual way. That percentage, together with other funds devoted to educational purposes, amounted to something like £400 a year. They had already purchased a large pair of globes for the instruction of the members, at a cost of about £20, and a large microscope for their amusement and instruction at a cost of £15. Opera glasses and other articles of that description had been purchased, and were lent out to members at the rate of twopence, whereas if they hired one at a theatre it would cost not less than a shilling. They had first-rate maps of all countries on the face of the globe, and the newsroom was well stocked with newspapers and periodicals, such as the *Quarterly Review*, *Cornhill Magazine*, *Westminster Review*, &c. Altogether they took in forty-four weekly newspapers and fourteen dailies. The number of volumes in the library was between 3,000 and 4,000. The Manufacturing Society had a capital of £58,000, 100 looms at work and 5,000 spindles. The new mill, at which they were about to set to work, was sixty-six yards long, five storeys high, and they were about to put down two 60-horsepower engines. They had expended on the building between £12,000 and £13,000, and on machinery and stock £21,000. When the mill was completed they expected to find work for 400 people, to pay wages at the rate of £18,000 a year, and they calculated that they would do a business of £75,000. The audience would see that this was all done by working men such as they, and they might do the same if they took the right course. The Rochdale Corn Mill, which Mr. Hadfield had referred to, had, according to the last account just concluded, a capital of £24,000. They had done a business during the quarter of £33,140, and realised profits to the amount of £2,665, turning out 760 sacks of flour per week. The audience would see that the people within themselves had power, and it was required that they should be made to know and feel it. The principal thing in such a business was confidence, and whenever Stalybridge members appointed their officers they must select men whom they thought were the best qualified to serve them; appoint them with full confidence, and exercise the necessary influence over them; and he (Mr. Greenwood) had no doubt they would succeed. If the people of Rochdale had had no confidence in each other they would not have succeeded in the manner they had, for it had been proved that there was more lost by people not having confidence in each other than otherwise.

Mr. Longfield said he came as a kind of messenger, bringing with him the good wishes of 700 members and friends, from the Manchester and Salford Society to those of the important and thriving town of Stalybridge. And why should not co-operators in one district cherish good wishes toward those in another? If it were right, and he was satisfied it was, for co-operators to combine for the pecuniary and general benefit of each other under the glorious name of co-operation, it was also right for such men and women who were at a distance to sympathise with efforts in the same direction all over the world. He referred to the new journal, the *Co-operator*, and hoped that all present would patronise it by becoming subscribers. It was a journal which advocated the system of co-operation; it contained accounts of all the societies in the country, and it would be of great importance to the members generally. Co-operation was not intended to set workman against employer, but rather to promote friendly feeling between them, and in several cases already it had been the means of preventing strikes. What was competition, which at present regulated all transactions, or nearly all ? It was a very peculiar thing ; it was quite interwoven with every custom of society ; and many employers would be glad if their business were conducted by some other system. It created suspicion and distrust, and those were two great evils, especially if they were allowed to grow. It went further ; it reduced healthy ambition to ignoble struggle. Instead of ambition being honest, it was often, under a system of competition, ignoble and dishonest, and then it became strife. It caused excessive riches on the one hand, which riches were confined to a very few, and excessive poverty on the other hand, which poverty was extended to the many. This ought not to be so, and something was wanted to bring about a different state of things. He believed co-operation would, if rightly understood and rightly applied, bring about the change. Co-operation, in the first place, enabled the working man to accumulate his savings gradually and easily. If the man joining a store was not well enough off to pay threepence or fivepence a week towards his shares out of his earnings, the very profits which he obtained at the end of every quarter would pay that threepence or fivepence for him, and more. Co-operation did a great deal, too, towards destroying the abominable system, the credit system. (Applause.) He believed those little shops—the " strap " shops—were the greatest enemies to working men, for instead of being beforehand they were always behindhand, and as soon as they received their earnings it was merely transferred from them to the shopkeeper for goods already consumed. It was therefore clear that a wonderful reformation in the habits and condition of the working classes was being effected by means of co-operative societies.

Mr. Marcroft then addressed the meeting. He was very happy indeed, he said, to see the Mayor of Stalybridge present. It had stimulated him to come from Oldham that night. He gave an outline of what the co-operators of Oldham were doing, and congratulated those of Stalybridge upon their endeavouring to form a library for the benefit of the members.

After a vote of thanks to the Mayor and its acknowledgment, the majority of the audience retired, the remainder staying to trip the light fantastic toe, which was kept up with great spirit until the last moment.

The following poem, which appears to be the work of an enthusiastic Stalybridge member, was published in the *Co-operator*, September, 1860 :—

CO-OPERATION.

All you who read this humble song,
 Whatever be your station,
Take our advice—you can't be wrong—
 Commence Co-operation.

You may have heard (we've often done)
 Of man's self-elevation ;
But all great victories must be won
 By warm Co-operation.

Should some vain despot scan this land,
 And threaten an invasion,
There's not a power on earth could stand
 Our firm Co-operation.

The monarch, seated on his throne,
 Boasts not self-preservation :
Weak our powers put forth alone ;
 Strong is Co-operation.

CO-OPERATION IN STALYBRIDGE.

You'll find by looking round about
    Upon the wide creation,
That God's designs are carried out
    By wise Co-operation.

The sun by day, the moon by night
    Shed forth illumination ;
One gives us heat, the other light,
    And hence Co-operation.

A lesson then for us to learn,
    For our own observation,
Is not another's help to scorn,
    But prize Co-operation.

Some selfish acts have lately come
    Before our observation,
Which only prompt a laugh from some
    Who love Co-operation.

While all are bound to do their best
    To raise a sodden nation,
Some *grocer's slaves* won't sell us yeast,
    To help Co-operation.

Such saddening conduct cannot harm,
    For here's our proclamation—
We've *got* a splendid, useful barm,
    By wise Co-operation.

Before we close, we may just state,
    By way of information,
That several of us have of late
    Commenced Co-operation.

Satan on heaven's high throne will sit,
    Lord of the whole creation,
Ere we will ask them for a bit
    To help Co-operation.

To pride ourselves on what we've done
    We feel we've great occasion ;
We've saved our " tin " since we begun
    With our Co-operation.

Old tradesmen view our efforts made
With awful consternation,
And, just because it spoils their trade,
They hate Co-operation.

I wish we had them on this spot,
To hear a smart oration,
Showing the blessings we have got
By our Co-operation.

Methinks I see them boiling o'er
With wrath and indignation ;
Bidding us halt, and say no more
About Co-operation.

Why sit and growl from day to day ?
Silence ! ye " Bulls of Basan,"
Lest " Balaam's Ass " should come and bray
Against Co-operation.

We're right ! and all the powers of hell,
In fiendish combination,
Can never toll the funeral knell
Of true Co-operation.

Our best advice to such we give,
Prepare for emigration ;
Our course is fixed, we mean to live
By our Co-operation.

Now we have done, we'll say no more,
But close this brief narration
By asking all to join some store,
And TRY Co-operation.

Stalybridge, July, 1860. S. S.

CHAPTER IV.

Another Year's Work—Four Branches Opened—A Year's Sales £42,114—1862 Annual Meeting—Effect of Cotton Panic—Co-operation in Stalybridge on its Trial.

ON the 29th June, 1861, a party and ball, in aid of the library, was held in the Foresters' Hall, Vaudrey Street. The Stalybridge Glee Club Concert Party and the Shepherds' Band were in attendance. Moses Hadfield, Esq., presided in the absence of the Mayor (Thomas Hadfield Sidebottom, Esq.). He said it was twelve months since they last met, and he thought the progress of the society during that time had been of a character that would be satisfactory to all concerned; indeed, he might congratulate them upon the very prosperous condition of the society. He said the amount of cash drawn over the counters during the year was £42,114. 12s. 7d., and the profit £2,848. 2s. 6d., which had been divided amongst the purchasers. Twelve months since the society had 800 members, now they numbered 2,000. During the year there had been four branch stores opened, namely, Castle Hall, Hurst, Waterloo, and Millbrook. The average weekly receipts at the branches were as follows :—Castle Hall, £299 ; Hurst, £110 ; Millbrook, £56 ; Waterloo, £55. During the past strike the society had been able to relieve the great distress of many of the poorer members, having paid in distressed cases alone upwards of £500. The largest amount of money drawn in one week was £1,300, which sum was taken during the week ended February 16th, 1861, and the smallest amount £750, taken during the strike. It appeared to him that the society was in a very prosperous condition, so much so that he thought it had surpassed their most sanguine expectations, considering that they had had a turnout to contend with, which some of the detractors of the society would say had a tendency to break it up. He thought the Stalybridge Co-operative Society stood in as favourable a position as any other society in the kingdom, and had every prospect of progressing on a more extensive scale. It was true they had some detractors, not only working men but others, and they could not expect to be exempt from that mode of censure. It seemed strange that opposition to the society should come from working men ; if it had come from some whom they might have considered as enemies, they could better have excused it, but from one of the workers he thought it came with a very bad grace. He did not think, however, that there was any danger to be feared from any kind of opposition ; the subject had been thoroughly ventilated, and the Stalybridge Co-operative Society was firmly established.

The third annual meeting was held in the Foresters' Hall on Tuesday evening, May 6th, 1862, when about 250 persons were present. Mr. R. Cobham was called upon to preside, and the twelfth quarterly report of the society was read. The lot of the people affected by strikes and by the cotton panic was such a hard one that the committee considered co-operation was upon its trial so far as Stalybridge was concerned. There were amongst the members, they said, many sincere co-operators—men who believed in the principles of the movement, and were determined to support them in times of adversity as well as prosperity. Take co-operation as a means of improving the social position of the workers, and there was no institution deserving of more cordial support. In the unparalleled state of the commercial world, they said, all must prepare to make some diminution in expenditure, in order to meet a lessened income. The earnings of the members had been reduced to a fractional part of what they were a year before, and it was found that those articles from which profit was derived had been almost entirely banished from the members' tables. The consequent falling off in the receipts at the various stores resulted in a reduced profit, which must be submitted to in hopes of better times.

The dividend on members' purchases for the quarter was 10d. in the £. The gross receipts for the quarter were £8,739. 12s. 6½d., and the profit £429. 18s. 9d.

The committee's report was unanimously adopted by the members, and the officers were elected as follows :—

Secretary—Thomas Baxter.
Treasurer—Johanan Booth.
Trustees—John France, James Batty, and William Harrison.
Auditors—George Hodgkinson and James Carter.

Committee—John Ridgway, George Rushton, Joseph Kinsey, Levi Wild, Joshua Allsop, and David Stringer.

The committee said they had caused proper balance sheets to be drawn up for each store, so that they could be told whether certain shops were making proper dividends. These balance sheets, however, were only intended for the use of the committee until they could draw up a satisfactory statement for the members, to be laid before a general or annual meeting. They thought it would not be wise to publish these balance sheets at present, because a store might pay a good dividend one quarter and an indifferent one the next; it would be better to obtain four quarterly balance sheets and strike average dividends. It was well known, however, that Waterloo Branch did not pay. If the members would use Rochdale flour, which could be obtained at the various stores, the dividend would be larger. The flour was dark because it was pure, and the Rochdale Pioneers sold none but this pure unadulterated article. Persons in the room had used it for several years, and that was a proof that the flour was good.

The meeting closed with a vote of thanks to the retiring officers.

The committee in their report for the thirteenth quarter, ended July 31st, 1862, said: " We cannot congratulate our members upon any increase of business. The great and prolonged depression which has fallen upon the cotton trade has already left its mark upon all connected with its various branches of manufacture, and especially upon the operatives. This will account to our members for the change in our hitherto progressive prosperity. The committee are making continued efforts to reduce the working expenses, and feel confident that the changes which are being made will tend to its permanent prosperity. The Waterloo Branch is no longer connected with the society, having been taken over by the members of that village at a valuation. We feel convinced that the business will be best and most profitably conducted when confined to the limits of the borough."

They reminded the members that it was their duty as well as interest to support the different departments, and that they were trading with themselves with their own capital. The committee assured the members that they, on their part, were adopting a policy of strict economy in all departments, and they hoped by that means, with the support of the members, to tide over the depression without impairing the interests of the society.

At this time the board room was in the Caroline Street premises, and monthly meetings of members were held there on first Monday evenings.

The quarter's sales were :—

	£	s.	d.
Water Street Grocery	2102	0	1
Castle Hall Branch	2088	11	0
Hurst Branch	766	10	0
Millbrook Branch	453	5	10½
Waterloo Branch	505	12	10½
	5915	19	10
Butchering	794	5	11
Drapery	219	17	0
	£6930	2	9

88   CO-OPERATION IN STALYBRIDGE.

The contributions to share capital were £285 and the withdrawals £775; £220 was paid as wages and £317 dividend and interest. The balance in hand at the opening of the quarter's accounts was £429; at the close, although the partial withdrawals of members who must have been hard pressed for money exceeded the contributions by £490, the balance was £242. A dividend of 6d. per £ on members' and non-members' purchases was declared, and there was a balance of £6. 19s. 9d. to carry forward. The balance sheet was as follows:—

	£	s.	d.
Members' Claims	3402	7	5
Interest	42	6	0
Reserve Fund	101	18	0½
Management Fund	33	0	8
Balance Profit	160	3	9
	£3739	15	10½

	£	s.	d.
Cash in hand	242	7	6½
Goods in stock	2754	4	5
Rochdale Corn Mill Society Shares	57	7	1
Fixed Stock	685	16	10
	£3739	15	10½

The *Ashton and Stalybridge Reporter* of August 16th, 1862, has a comment that the society was considered to be passing through the cotton panic tolerably well, and that doubtless upon the resumption of activity it would enjoy a good share of prosperity. Dividend was paid at three places, including two of the branches, those at Hurst and Waterloo. The butchering department was closed on Monday afternoons, and the grocery on Wednesdays at 2 o'clock. Drapery was closed on Mondays, Tuesdays, Wednesdays, and Thursdays at 7, and Fridays at 8, but was kept open until 10 p.m. on Saturdays.

On Thursday, September 4th, 1862, Mr. James Hyde, general manager, tendered his resignation, which was accepted by the committee, and the *Ashton and Stalybridge Reporter* of September 20th, 1862, remarks that one of the signs of the times was to be found in the fact that the co-operative society had advertised for a manager, and that no less than sixty persons had applied for the vacant situation.

CHAPTER V.

DISSENSION—RESIGNATION OF OFFICERS—STRUGGLING DEPARTMENTS—SOCIETY OWNS A DOG—RUMOURS CIRCULATED BY OPPONENTS—VOTE OF CONFIDENCE.

ON Monday evening, September 15th, 1862, a special meeting of members was held in the Court Room, Town Hall, about 500 members being present. Unusual interest was shown in the meeting from the fact that a handbill had been extensively circulated in the town, stating that the committee were ruining the society. Another bill had been placed on the window shutters of the draper's shop in Caroline Street, which read as follows:—" Notice. This shop is closed by order of the Committee of Mismanagement," and was signed by "One of the old committee."

Mr. W. Roberts was called upon to preside, and at the outset he stated that no speaker would be allowed more than five minutes at a time, nor to address the meeting more than twice on any one subject. Acting on these regulations, a good number were able to give expression to their opinions.

The Chairman said that the first business was to

THE COMMITTEE, 1862 TO 1864.

J. HACKETT, JOHN RIDGWAY, JOSEPH KINSEY, ROBERT COBHAM, SAMUEL HADFIELD, Sec'ETARY, JAMES LAWTON, W. ROBERTS, GEO. RUSHTON, W. HARRISON, CHAS. JONES, MAT. HUTCHISON, J. BAMFORD, D. STRINGER, Chairman.

consider the proffered resignation of Mr. Johanan Booth as treasurer. A letter had been received from Mr. Gartside, a solicitor, of Ashton, stating that the treasurer's books must be examined before the 16th inst., as he was retiring from office. It appears that there were differences between the committee, treasurer, and secretary. The last named had already retired. It was reported that the treasurer had stated that he had more than £200 in his hands which the books of the society "did not credit him with," and the chairman announced at the meeting that the committee had not been able to get a balance sheet from him. The chairman thought the resignation ought to be accepted.

The reading of some of these early records reminds the writer of the mistaken attitude that is occasionally taken up by very worthy men in positions of trust. In one instance a gentleman in such a position became very indignant when he was asked by auditors to prove a balance of cash that he stated he had in hand. In these days of more advanced accounting and more thorough audit such instances are rare, however, and the requirements of auditors who are capable in their profession do not in the least ruffle the feathers of the accounting party.

A member asked if, by resigning, Mr. Booth would throw off his liability to the society. He had been in office from the infancy of the society, and the shops, &c., were in his name, one of them being held on a lease for seven years. He would like to know, too, whether in the event of Mr. Booth withdrawing his capital it would be right to allow his name to be retained in the rent books, &c.

Another member inquired if they really could appoint another treasurer, seeing that Mr. Booth was the tenant of the shops.

One of the committee, in reply, stated that no member could throw off any liability to the society until he had been left two years. The positions of treasurer and tenant of shops were distinct. They could accept his resignation of the office of treasurer and still retain his name in the rent books if they thought proper.

Another matter they had to report to that meeting, the chairman said, was that the committee had determined to have the times of all their servants kept, such times to be paid for at rates per week. They had found that the butchering department did not pay, and a change of management had been made. Two of the committee had attended the previous week to assist the new butcher, with the result that 3s. in the £ had been realised. Mr. Marsland had bought them four beasts last week, and the butchering department was looking up under its new management; in fact, when they closed the shop at 8 o'clock the previous Saturday night they had sold more beef than had ever been sold before. The drapery department, which had been closed for a time, was opened for a few hours last week end, with the result that £6 was drawn. It was their intention to open it every Saturday in future. This was proceeding in the right direction, and with the co-operation of the members the society would become prosperous and pay a good dividend.

The resignation of Mr. Booth was then accepted, and Mr. James Lawton was appointed in his place. Mr.

Charles Jones, of Stalybridge, and Mr. Luke Thornley, of Hurst, were elected to the committee.

The chairman stated that examination had been made of the various shops, and they were improving the control. They also found that they possessed more property than they had been aware of, for on looking over the bills it was found that they were paying tax for a large Newfoundland dog, which had been named " Dividend." They had not bought the dog, and had never seen the schedule under which it was taxed until four days after it was too late to appeal. If they had to pay tax for it, however, he presumed it belonged to them, and would like to know what they were to do with it. (Cries of " Drown it.") He was glad to find that the men of Hurst were doing their duty. They had formed a sub-committee to look after the interests of the branch, and the store had been thoroughly cleaned. One or two of the mills in Hurst had gone on full time, and the receipts had considerably increased, £120 having been drawn over the counter last week.

Mr. Cobham substantiated the statements of the chairman, and said he had been appointed to look after the various shops until a general manager could be appointed, and, as the shopmen did not like him, they had named him " Inspector Cobham."

A member then referred to various representations and rumours which were being extensively circulated in the town for the purpose of inducing members to withdraw their capital, and reminded them to be on their guard and work together for their own good. It had been said that it was no light matter to be a member of the committee, for there was a good deal of anxiety in reference to the business of the society. Members were withdrawing their capital because of bad times, and, in a few instances, as a result of the misrepresentations of interested parties. If the capital of the society was withdrawn to any considerable amount, then the fixed stock would become to them nothing more in value than old timber. There would be loss also on capital sunk in trade stocks, which could not be disposed of until the cotton trade improved. A sum of £1,000 was sunk in drapery, and if members could purchase it, all would be well there; and the drapery stock might yet prove a good investment, owing to the great rise in prices since it was purchased.

It was unanimously resolved—" That the committee possess the full confidence of the members, and are empowered to obtain legal advice on any subject which may arise in connection with the present position of the society."

During the speaker's remarks a dog was heard barking very loudly, and considerable amusement was created by someone calling, " Yond's co-op. dog."

Another member said he had heard a report that the committee received a shilling for every hour they sat. (Cries of " It's false.") He knew it was false, but thought he would mention it. He was quite sanguine about the future of the society, and if members were compelled to withdraw their capital, he would borrow in accordance with the rules. He was confident the committee were the right men in the right place, and should support them.

The meeting shortly afterwards broke up, having

lasted about two hours and a half. Stormy scenes had been expected, but, on the contrary, the members were unanimous in supporting the committee, and it was demonstrated that there were sufficient zealous and warm-hearted friends of co-operation in the society to carry it through its difficulties and make it thereafter a powerful society.

The society was first registered under the Industrial and Provident Societies Act of 1852. At that time there was no such thing as limited liability, the Limited Liability Act being passed some three years later, in 1855, and several times amended in 1856-7-8. In the event of a winding-up, every member of the society would have been liable down to his last penny until creditors were satisfied. The protection of the new Act was sought in 1862, a meeting of members held in the Court Room of the Town Hall on the 29th September deciding that the society be enrolled under the Limited Liability Act.

In the *Co-operator* for March, 1862, there appears the following paragraph :—

> STALYBRIDGE.—There has been some falling-off here of late, but not to an alarming extent. This should cheer the members up, and induce them to persevere in well-doing. The eleventh quarterly report shows the receipts to have been £10,591, reserve fund £98, dividend 1s. to members and 6d. to non-members.

A falling-off is scarcely the thing to cheer up the members. Probably the writer of the paragraph meant that things might have been worse, and that members should not be discouraged, but rather stirred or inspired to hold on. The thirteenth report, showing a decrease of over £3,000 from the figures quoted by the *Co-operator*, has already been referred to, and it will be seen as the story is unfolded that there were still greater difficulties to face, when other branches were to secede, and a quarter's sales were to fall below two thousand pounds, grim evidence of the struggles and suffering of the people under that almost overwhelming adversity, the Cotton Panic.

The report for the fourteenth quarter, ended 31st October, 1862, is the first in which the word " Limited " is used as the last of the society's name, thus indicating that the application for registry with limited liability had been successful. The report is as follows :—

> The committee are happy that they are enabled now to publish a full and correct account of the real condition of the society (which they are convinced has never been done before). It may be fairly inferred that it has now successfully passed through its infantine diseases, and we therefore feel confident that it will flourish and pay dividends ; that will satisfy and benefit its members, confound and disappoint its enemies, and make certain individuals blush and shame that it not only survives, but that it actually prospers, after their flagrant attempts to overthrow it.
>
> Your committee are sorry that they cannot pay any dividend this time ; yet they are confident that when you compare the last report and the present you will find a sufficient reason why.
>
> Millbrook and Hurst members have taken their stores at a fair valuation, and are now on their own responsibility.

A comparison of the two quarters' accounts reveals the influence of the Cotton Panic on the society's trade, and on the condition of its members. The Water Street grocery sales had decreased from £2,102 the previous quarter to £1,774, Grosvenor Street £2,088

CO-OPERATION IN STALYBRIDGE.

to £1,685, Hurst £766 to £763, and Millbrook £453 to £412; butchering from £794 to £669, and drapery £219 to £105. The total sales, July quarter, were £6,930, in October they had fallen to £5,411. The severance of Waterloo Branch three months before would account for something like £500 of the decrease.

Mr. John Ashcroft, a member of the Board of Management of the present Waterloo Society, has obtained some information as to the formation of the Waterloo Branch. As far as he can ascertain, he says, Mr. Samuel Robinson was engineer at Jamieson's mill in Dukinfield, where now stand the Compo Works of Messrs. Hy. Shaw and Co. Mr. Robinson came in contact with the co-operators of Stalybridge and induced them to form the branch at Waterloo. When the co-operators there became established as another society, Mr. Robinson was a member of the committee, and remained on the Board for many years. The first manager to the new Waterloo Society was Mr. Joseph Hadfield, who afterwards joined the Church of England Ministry, and who has been for a long time vicar of Hadfield.

The "General Statement" of October 31st, 1862, reads:—

GENERAL STATEMENT.

Liabilities.	£	s.	d.
Members' Claims, as per Ledger	2695	13	11
Interest	76	1	0
Reserve Fund	Cannot be		
Management Fund	found.		
	£2771	14	11

Assets.	£	s.	d.
Cash in Hand	381	14	5½
Goods in Stock	1563	8	6
Invested in the R.C.M.S.	69	4	4
Fixed Stock Account	608	7	2
	2622	14	5¾
By Loss	149	0	5½
	£2771	14	11

Note the concise announcement of the non-existence of the reserve and management funds.

CHAPTER VI.

Hath hope been smitten in its early dawn ?
Have clouds o'ercast thy purpose, trust, or plan ?
Have faith, and struggle on !
—*R. S. S. Andros.*

1863-4—SALES STILL LOWER, BUT A BETTER BALANCE SHEET—
1S. 6D. DIVIDEND—EDUCATION AND " THE CO-OPERATOR "
—NO DIVIDEND—A CROWDED MEETING—BUSINESS TRANS-
FERRED TO GROSVENOR STREET—MEMBERS OF COMMITTEE
RESIGN — PROPOSAL TO BUY PROPERTY — BUTCHERING
GIVEN UP—ONE GROCER'S AND ONE DRAPER'S SHOP ONLY
LEFT.

THE committee, auditors, treasurer, manager, and all employés of the society, together with a number of members, met on Tuesday evening, January 6th, 1863. Supper was served and a very pleasant evening spent. It was said that such meetings proved that the society, which of late had passed through a series of changes, was progressing favourably, and would soon be placed upon a sound and permanent basis.

In their report for the quarter ended 30th September, 1863, the committee said they had great pleasure in being able to state that the business was steadily progressing in spite of the severe strain upon the resources of the members during the preceding two years. The report continued :—

> After numberless vicissitudes and changes, we feel that the interests of our society are consolidated, and that it is now upon a firm and sound basis.
>
> The receipts during the last quarter would, no doubt, have allowed a greater division of profits than the committee deem advisable to be paid under present circumstances. Guided by past experience, we are assured that the true and safe interests of your society depend upon being at all times able to meet its engagements with promptitude, and not to feel crippled or doubtful of our financial position. It is this view of the society's interests that has determined your committee upon the division of profits to be paid at the present time.
>
> With regard to the future of this society, the committee look forward with a sanguine hope to better days, when each share will become as valuable as those in the most prosperous societies.

The separation of Hurst and Millbrook members would reduce the quarter's sales perhaps £1,000 ; the decrease was nearly £2,000—from £5,411 to £3,476. Strangely enough, drapery sales had more than doubled, £234 compared with £105, the decrease being in grocery and butchering, the only other departments. The statement of liabilities and assets certainly forms better reading than that of a year before. Fixed stock appears £63 less, whilst the total assets are £148 more, and instead of a loss there is shown a profit of £184. A dividend of a 1s. to members and 6d. to non-members was declared. Messrs. William Moores and Nathaniel Moss were the auditors.

Three months later the committee expressed their gratification at the fact that the business was marked by constancy and firmness, and that the profits would enable them to pay a larger dividend. Eighteenpence to members and a 1s. to non-members were declared, and fixed stock was considerably further reduced. When they reflected upon the state of trade, they said, the difficulty which some of the members had had to pass through, and the self-denial which all had been forced to practise, they were assured that the report would be both cheering and acceptable. The balance sheet was signed by Samuel Hadfield, secretary.

Although we do not find evidence of much progress of the newsroom and library referred to at the 1860 and 1861 gatherings, it is clear that the committee and secretary did not forget the educational side of our movement. The Cotton Panic would preclude the setting apart of a fund in Stalybridge, but they appear to have thought that the object could be achieved in another way. In the *Co-operator* of July, 1864, the following appears :—

> STALYBRIDGE ("GOOD INTENT INDUSTRIAL").—We hope that the good feeling shown towards your publication will result in its continuance, and tend to its prosperity, and that *The Co-operator* will become the household paper of every true friend to progress among the industrial classes. In your last issue it is suggested that *The Co-operator* should become more varied in its character, and embrace other matters than mere reports of the progress of these societies. This suggestion meets with our approval, and we think, if carried out, will make *The Co-operator* a useful and attractive publication. It must be remembered that many persons who become members of these useful societies are men who have moved in the lower strata of society; such men need instruction as well as encouragement, and your paper may become to some of them a pioneer to more elevated tasks, and a guide to a better social existence.
> SAMUEL HADFIELD, Secretary.

CO-OPERATION IN STALYBRIDGE.

The half-yearly meeting, held Tuesday, November 1st, 1864, was a crowded one, owing to the fact that there was no dividend to declare, and to a report which had been circulated that the general manager had been discharged. Mr. Charles Jones, who was voted to the chair, said his position was a disagreeable one, but he would endeavour to act fairly and honestly to all. It had unfortunately happened that at every annual meeting during the society's history they had had someone to vilify or condemn. Two years ago it led to a separation; twelve months ago it was a butcher who had to be condemned, and now he understood it was the committee or someone else who was in for it because there was no dividend. It appears there had been, as Mr. Jones hinted, a separation two years before, the seceding members setting up as a joint-stock concern in Grosvenor Square, next door, on the High Street side, to the shop which, in its improved state, is now occupied by the society's tailoring department.

The secretary read the report, which was, briefly, as follows :—

> In presenting you with another quarterly report, the committee are not prepared to say that the society is in the position which they have been labouring for some time to attain. We find from the auditors' report on the past quarter's business that there has been a decided loss. To account for this state of things we must confess that we are not, as a committee, prepared to accept the full responsibility. It is evident that there has been wrong somewhere, and we can at present only point to the figures with a feeling of disappointment, and hope, by a change of management, to make this society what others are, a decided success. We feel that this state of things in connection with our society is far from satisfactory, and

CO-OPERATION IN STALYBRIDGE.   105

that there must be at once a curtailment of expenditure in rent, taxes, &c., before we can secure that amount of dividend which members have a right to expect.

The financial statement showed the liabilities to be as follows :—Members' claims as per members' ledger £2,426, interest £58, accounts owing £474, loan £56. Proportion of rates, gas, water, insurance, and licenses £20. The assets were returned as cash in hand £299, goods in stock £2,015, invested in Rochdale Corn Mill £27, fixed stock £479, a deficiency of £214. The report from the auditors was read as follows :—

> In compliance with the rules, we make a report of our audit to this half-yearly meeting. We found the books neatly and properly entered up, with the exception of a few errors which were rectified. One was an error of 10d. in the petty cash book against the secretary. We have given him credit for it in the present quarter's accounts. We found proper vouchers for items entered in the cash book, both on the Dr. and Cr. sides, and that such vouchers prove that the balance of cash in hand, named in the report, is correct. The auditors thought it necessary the previous quarter, to give more satisfaction to them, and to the members, that the treasurer should on the last day in each quarter pay the whole of his cash into the bank, so that the bank book would be a guarantee to them that the secretary's balance was correct. This has been done this quarter, and the balance to our credit in the bank on that day, together with a few relief tickets, corresponds with the balance in the cash book. The committee have at different times borrowed money on interest from members, and we are sorry to add that these amounts were not entered properly in the ledger, in consequence of which an error of £31 too little was made in the liabilities last quarter. It was necessary in the same quarter to get a new ledger for members' private accounts, and in transferring the accounts from the old ledger to the new, two

or three mistakes, amounting to abont £11, occurred, which made members' claims appear that amount more than they really were ; this was favourable to the society, and reduced the previous error to £20, which has been counterbalanced by keeping fixed stock at its previous amount. We beg to ask, for the good of the members, and for the accuracy of the accounts, that members send their books in every quarter, to be examined and checked by the auditors. We often find these books a great help in keeping the accounts straight. We should be pleased if we had nothing more serious to lay before the meeting, but it has transpired that an error of considerable amount was made in the June report. Bills owing, instead of reading £48. 10s. 6d., as stated in the report, should have been about £200.

Several questions were asked as to the profits made at the Castle Hall and Water Street shops, the responsibility for the accuracy of the stocktaking, and the attitude of the committee toward the manager. It appears that an unfortunate disagreement had arisen ; some of the committee were for and some against the manager, and the members also were divided, at least one asserting that the committee were prejudiced against one whom they had reason to trust. One cause of the difference was a purchase of boots and shoes to the value of £49 by the manager. The committee thought he should have consulted them before buying the goods, and when they told him so he resented their attitude, saying that if he were to be their manager he would not ask their consent in such matters. Another cause was his action in employing a lady in the drapery department who had not been appointed by the committee, and in spite of remonstrance from them. There was a motion that the action of the committee be confirmed, and an amendment that the manager be reinstated. At this point a discussion arose as to whether women should vote. It was said that many members had brought their wives in order that they also might vote. It was decided that women could vote if they were members and had no husbands. Tellers were appointed and the motion was carried by a large majority.

Mr. John Bamford said that when the committee found there was no dividend they tried for days to find the cause and that accounted for the report being delayed. Every member of the committee was a member of the society, and had as much interest in a good dividend as any other member; each sacrificed a good deal of time in watching the interests of the society, and was as anxious as anybody for its success. He had examined past balance sheets and found that for the last six quarters the income had been about the same per quarter; they had paid no more for wages, rent, taxes, &c., this quarter than in any previous one, and, therefore, when there was no dividend there was something wrong. He could not tell where, he only wished he could. The previous dividends averaged more than 1s. in the pound. He was sorry they were £200 behind nothing, and that there was little prospect of a future dividend, but he hoped there would be no more "splits," or co-operation in Stalybridge would be done for. If they were true co-operators they were so from principle, and as such he advised them to look at things in a fair and proper light. Since the society commenced £5,500 had been paid to its members, a fact which spoke volumes; let them stick to co-operation, and if any careless, reckless management got amongst them, let it be driven out, and the society would again flourish. (Applause.)

It was then resolved almost unanimously—"That the whole of the stores be transferred to Castle Hall premises."

A requisition was handed to the chairman, signed by twenty members, calling a special meeting of the society to be held the following week for the purpose of "discharging and electing fresh officers," and the meeting then broke up, having lasted $3\frac{1}{2}$ hours.

The special meeting was held on Tuesday evening, November 8th, 1864, in the Courtroom of the Town Hall. Mr. John Ridgway was unanimously appointed to preside. He said the meeting was called by a requisition of twenty members, and he would like some of them to get up and state what their object was in calling them together that night.

After a lengthy pause, Mr. J. Swift said that as one who had signed the requisition, he had to state that he had done so from the fact that at the last meeting the committee did not seem to be as friendly with one another as men engaged in such a noble work as co-operation ought to be, and he thought that if the meeting was held it would give any member of the committee a chance, and if there were any who ought to resign, they could ask them to do so, and he had no doubt they would comply. Several of the requisitionists having expressed themselves similarly, Mr. Kinsey and Mr. Chas. Jones tendered their resignations, which were accepted, and Mr. Marshall Ashworth and Mr. Geo. Storrs were elected in their stead. Another

Central Grocery.—Grosvenor Street.

member of the committee, Mr. W. Roberts, was accused of " having gone about trying to prejudice the members against the late manager " by one outspoken member, who objected to Mr. Roberts being returned to the committee for that reason, and because the committee came forward and said they were not prepared to take the responsibility for the position of the society. Twelve members voted against, but there was a forest of hands held up for Mr. Roberts, and he was re-elected. The same outspoken member, whom we will call Mr. B., asserted that while the society drew more money than others it was a long way behind them in dividend. Mr. Cobham said he lived in Ashton, and could not properly attend to his duties. He would resign, and move that Mr. B. be elected in his place. Here there were loud cries of " We won't have him ; we've had enough of him." Mr. B. said he had no desire for office, but he was as strongly in favour of co-operation as anyone, and he could assure them that his reason for acting as he had was that he wished the society to prosper and pay as good dividends as any other. He would not accept office. It was then moved—"That the committee as at present constituted retain office." This was at once seconded by a score or two of voices, and upon being put was carried with only two or three against.

Mr. Hutchinson said he would be glad if the society could pay 20s. in the pound, and personally he would be willing to sacrifice his dividend and interest until they attained that position. The Chairman said there appeared to be considerable uneasiness about Water Street Branch being closed, but it could not be avoided, and all true co-operators would put up with it. Mr. Kinsey said that £49 below the average for the quarter was taken at the stores.

The Chairman said he would like to know the opinion of the members about buying some property, so that they could live under their own vine and fig tree. Mr. R. Greenwood said he was in favour of a large business in cheap premises and as few servants as possible. He was willing to sacrifice interest and dividend in order to purchase some property, and he thought that if the society had not funds it would be desirable to issue special shares for such a purpose. Mr. Henry Hurst said that, in order to test the opinion of the meeting, he would move—"That the committee be empowered to enter into negotiations for the purchase of some shop property."

Mr. Kinsey thought they had better not attempt to buy property until their shares were worth 20s. in the pound, and Mr. Chas. Jones said it was ridiculous to talk of buying property when they were insolvent. Mr. R. Greenwood remarked that if every house in Stalybridge had to be paid for before it were built there would be very few dwellings in the town.

The motion was then put and carried by a large majority, and Mr. G. Storrs moved a vote of thanks to those members of the committee who had resigned. The Chairman said he could testify to the energy, zeal, and ability with which Mr. Kinsey had attended to his duties, and Mr. Cobham spoke in a similar manner of Mr. Jones's labours. A lady member said there could be no doubt that Mr. Jones and Mr. Kinsey had both done their duty. She wished the servants of the society would be more civil to their customers, and related how she went to the store, and because she tasted the butter with a half-crown which she had in her hand, she was insulted ; such conduct ought to be put a stop to, if the society must prosper. The motion was unanimously carried. Mr. Kinsey returned thanks, and said he hoped they would be content without dividend until they were worth 20s. in the pound.

The difficulties of the years 1861 to 1864 had brought about the secession of three of the four branches, and they proved too much for butchering, which was given up in 1864. At the end of that year there were grocery and drapery only, with one shop for each department.

Mr. Watson had succeeded Mr. Rowbotham as manager.

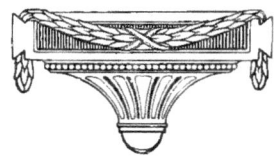

CHAPTER VII.

Hope on, hope ever ! though to-day be dark,
The sweet sunburst may smile on thee to-morrow.
—*Gerald Massey.*

1865—INFLUENCE OF COTTON PANIC STILL EVIDENT—CO-OPERATION'S " HOUR OF NEED "—LOSSES—MANY STEADFAST MEMBERS—AGAIN A SHILLING DIVIDEND—TWO SHOPS OWNED—THE DARK DAYS PASSING.

IN April, 1865, the committee published a report and accounts covering six months. The sales for the first half of the period, to December 31st, 1864, were £2,208, compared with £3,605, December, 1863 ; and for the quarter ended March 31st, 1865, they were £1 860 only. The report reads :—

> The committee beg to express their sincere thanks to the members who have shown their confidence in, and given their support to, co-operation in its hour of need. In the last report you found a balance loss of £214, which would doubtless surprise and dishearten even the most sanguine of our members. If we compare the last with some of the preceding quarters, we can only conclude that there has been some gross mismanagement at the least, for the receipts have been nearly equal for five quarters

successively, including the last, the 21st. In the 17th, 18th, 19th, and 20th quarters we made very respectable profits, and how it should happen that we could make those profits and then make a loss at the rate of £214 in one quarter, with about the same receipts, is more than your committee can at present account for. For instance, let us compare the 18th and 21st quarters' receipts and profits. There is a difference in the receipts of £4 only; yet there is shown a profit one quarter of £249, and a loss the other of £214. We think even those who have taken umbrage at our giving up Water Street Store, concentrating our trade, curtailing expenses in rents, wages, &c., will, upon mature reflection, conclude that we have adopted the only feasible, sure, and practical plan for restoring confidence and establishing the society upon a firm basis, by purchasing property and making the shareholders safe in their investments; and we are convinced that when we are freed from all the old encumbrances and settled in our own premises we shall be able to pay reasonable dividends; and then, we hope, bring back the members who have ceased to trade with us, who by that time will have seen the folly of building up a society one day, and pulling it down the day following.

Mr. Joseph Greenwood was secretary at this time. In the 24th quarterly report, July, 1865, the committee congratulated the members on being able to pay a dividend of 1s. in the pound to members and 9d. to non-members, besides finishing off a debt of £57, owing at the end of the previous quarter. They had about six hundred members who possessed more than two thousand shares. The society owned two shops and some outbuildings in Grosvenor Street, which cost £462. 17s. 6d., and the committee stated that they were in hopes that if the members would trade at their own shops the society would become thoroughly prosperous and once more pay good dividends.

On Wednesday evening, November 1st, 1865, the half-yearly meeting was held in the Courtroom of the Town Hall, about eighty members being present. Mr. Matthew Hutchinson was called upon to preside, and after a few remarks from him, Mr. Joseph Greenwood, secretary, read the report, from which the following is extracted :—

In presenting this report, the committee confess their pleasure in thanking the real, steadfast, and persevering members for their unshaken fidelity in the cause of co-operation, and their commiseration for, and sympathy with, the unstable, dissatisfied non-trading ones ; they contend that as a committee they are justified in sympathising with those who are thoroughly convinced of the great advantages of co-operation, yet who (in the face of these convictions, either to serve party purposes, satisfy vindictive feelings, or something worse) can allow themselves to be made into the most useful instruments, or willing tools, to frustrate, to overthrow, and if possible, to annihilate co-operation. For this reason the committee feel it an imperative duty to speak out, to tell the members and the public, that many of the originators of this society, who advocated it in the strongest terms, who invested money in it, and advised others to do so, who worked for it soon and late, and never thought they had done too much, that many such members have deserted it, and that now they strive to injure it ! What inconsistency ! what consummate folly ! ! what complete madness ! ! ! to originate, to advocate, to support, to defend, and work for a society a time, and then because they cannot have exactly their own way, to turn round and pull down their own pet hobby. Now we beg of those members to reconsider the matter, to banish such narrow-mindedness, to do justice to themselves, to come again to us and sit down with us under our own vine and fig tree, for we are now in our own shop, which is respectable, comfortable, and convenient. There is room for all, and we do most sincerely invite every member to enjoy the benefits, taste the sweets, and gather the fruits of co-operation. We beg also to inform the members that we should be glad to take up shares, at the late prices, from non-trading members, and we trust that they will either embrace this favourable opportunity of selling out, or commence trading with us at once, and cease to be drones, sucking out the heart's core from the busy hive of industry.

The financial statement showed that the cash received during the quarter had been about £2,000, while the dividend was declared to be 1s. in the £ upon members' purchases, and 10d. in the £ upon non-members'.

The report was passed unanimously, and several suggestions were thrown out for still further improving the extending business of the society, after which a vote of thanks was tendered to the chairman.

The general feeling was expressed that the dark hours of the society were passed, and that in future it would go on in a manner thoroughly satisfactory to all concerned.

The closing times for shops from the 5th November, 1865, were :—Mondays and Wednesdays, 8 p.m.; Tuesdays, 2 p.m.; Thursdays, Fridays, and Saturdays, 9 p.m. On Wakes days the same year the shops were closed at 2 p.m. Monday and Wednesday, and at 8 p.m. Tuesday.

There is a reminder in the records here of the days when tremendous puncheons, &c., of some grocery goods were bought and sold. It was arranged in November, 1865, that all tierces and other packages too heavy to be weighed on the premises be dealt with at the railway station. In the same year another article that we do not now find in our shops was bought from Mr. Sykes—a sugar-chopping machine.

On Saturday, December 2nd, 1865, a tea party in connection with the society was held in the People's Institute, Plantation Ground, about 400 persons being present. After tea, the Mayor, James Sidebottom, Esq., occupied the chair, and was supported on the platform by many warm-hearted friends of the co-operative movement. The Chairman, in opening the meeting, said he had gladly responded to the kind invitation of the committee to preside on that occasion. He should, however, say very little, as he was surrounded by gentlemen who had made co-operation their study, and whose opinions were entitled to more consideration than his own. He suggested that the addresses should be short and sweet, as he knew that many of them would rather listen to the strains of the band, and join in the festive dance, than to long speeches. He had been highly gratified to hear from the report of the society that they had got through their trials and difficulties and that their affairs had been placed upon what was no doubt a better, because a firmer, basis. He considered that working men were justified in forming these societies, and if they appointed managers who would attend to their business, so that people could buy their goods at a fair market price, there would be no doubt that, to use a common remark, it would " bring grist to the mill," and that would give them good dividends. It appeared that in the past all had not been straight sailing, but he trusted that in the future the society would make a stand, and attain a position equal to others of the same class throughout the country. (Cheers.)

The Rev. T. Floyd said he could not avoid expressing

his personal gratification at seeing such a mixed assembly, neither could he avoid saying that he felt strongly on the subject of co-operation. He rejoiced at the progress of every movement which had for its aim the improvement and elevation of working men. It was a fact that no class could get on without co-operation, and no matter whether a man was rich or poor, he was dependent upon co-operation. He knew the Stalybridge Society had had great difficulties to grapple with, but he thought that, with the improved state of the town, the members would be able to draw a better dividend. If working men were not content no other class of the community would be content, and as the spread of co-operation would tend to make them more prosperous, contented, and happy, it deserved the support of all good men. Upon these and other grounds he gladly availed himself of the opportunity of being with them on that occasion.

Mr. Thomas Hodson remarked that he had heard of a certain society in the town where, if in the audit of the accounts any difficulty arose, it was coolly said : " Sup, an' it'll be reet." As one of the auditors of the Stalybridge Co-operative Society, he could say that such was not the case with their accounts, for they were found right without a single " sup." He considered Mr. Joseph Greenwood, the secretary, to be the right man in the right place ; he was kind, and was always ready with whatever information was required, and was a most valuable servant of the society.

The Rev. J. P. Hopps, in the course of his remarks, said he had laboured under a misapprehension with regard to the meeting, for whilst he expected to find it a meeting of men, it was composed partly of women. He might, however, have expected to find it composed of women, for, after all, co-operation had most to do with women, for while the men worked for the money, the women spent it. (Laughter.) He had been thinking a great deal about co-operation during the day, and it had been in his thoughts so much that he was almost afraid he should be preaching about it on the following Sunday. He might have many a worse subject for a text, for what better could a parson preach or talk about than the homes of working people, and how they could improve those homes by means of co-operation. There was a charm about the word "Co-operation," when properly understood. "Co" meant "with one another," and "operation" meant "work," so that the word really meant "work with one another." He was a believer in co-operation; the movement was not simply a selfish one, but it appeared to him to be a great means of educating the people. Give a man a share in the bank, or a co-operative society, and that very minute he became much more of a man. If fifty men were united for an object, they had different ideas and passions, and they had to learn how to moderate their feelings and govern their passions—in fact, to learn how to be men. Co-operation was a greater question than Parliamentary reform, and he hoped to have the privilege shortly of speaking to working men on that which would tend so much to improve and elevate them in the social scale.

Mr. Henry Pitman, editor of the *Co-operator*, next addressed the meeting. He said there was great food for thought in what had been advanced by the various speakers. He was pleased to find them assembled in such a fine and noble room, devoted to educational advancement of the people, for co-operation could only advance in proportion to the education of the people. The speaker went on to describe the various virtues of co-operation, and especially named honesty in word and deed, cash dealings, and a firm belief that the principles of co-operation were true. Referring to the number of ladies present, he expressed a wish that all their partners had been with them, but he was afraid he had seen some of them rambling the streets with their pipes in their mouths, and their hands in their pockets. Reference had been made by one of the speakers to " snuggeries," but those who lived in glass houses should not throw stones. He must be faithful with them, and tell them candidly it was to their shame that they could not have a party like that without a stall for the sale of liquors. There was a real danger in having such a stall, and he must say that with one exception he had never found such a thing before in connection with co-operation.

Mr. John Ridgway next addressed the meeting, and in the course of a thoroughly practical address, showed that during the last twenty-five years innumerable schemes had been propounded for improving the working classes. Working men had a right to combine and lay out their money to the best advantage. Co-operation was yet in its infancy, for persons did not become true co-operators by simply joining a co-operative society; it was not true co-operation for a woman, when she went to the stores to expect her goods for nothing, and a good dividend into the bargain, as some women in Stalybridge expected. True co-operation had faith in the manager of the societies buying in the best markets, and unless they had that faith they had a great deal to learn before they were true co-operators. It was true there had been much in Stalybridge to disturb that faith, but it was again becoming firmer, as was evidenced from the fact that during the present quarter they were drawing more money by £31 per week at their shop in Grosvenor Street than they were previously drawing at the whole of the branches. With some pertinent advice to lady co-operators, as well as non-co-operators, the speaker concluded his address.

Votes of thanks were tendered to the gentlemen who had responded to the invitation of the committee, and to the mayor for presiding.

CHAPTER VIII.

Say not the struggle nought availeth,
The labor and the wounds are vain.
—*A. H. Clough.*

1866 TO 1868—STEADY PROGRESS—INTERESTING ADDRESSES BY THE REVS. J. P. HOPPS AND J. R. STEPHENS—SHARES AT PAR—SHOPMEN'S BONUS SYSTEM—TAILORING AGENCIES TAKEN UP—REPRESENTED AT ANNUAL CONFERENCE—"REPORTER" ACCOUNT OF CHEQUERED CAREER AND THE GREAT CHANGE—MR. J. RIDGWAY BECOMES TREASURER.

IN their twenty-seventh quarterly report, April, 1866, the committee congratulated the members on the steady and increased progress and stability of the society, and hoped that all true, earnest, and well-wishing members would reciprocate.

They were confident that as the great crisis in the cotton trade had passed, greater results might be realised by the members purchasing all they could at the society's stores, and said that unless they did, they could not receive, nor reasonably expect, the same benefits as members belonging to similar societies who were heart and soul in the great work of social redemption. The dividend for the quarter was 1s. 3d. in the £ to members, and 1s. to non-members. The annual meeting was held on Tuesday evening, May 1st, 1866, in the Court Room of the Town Hall, Mr. John Bamford presiding. The attendance was not large, but the greatest unanimity prevailed. The report was unanimously passed, and Messrs. M. Ashworth, R. Whittle, J. Hampshire, H. Kenworthy, and J. Kay were elected to the committee. The three first named were re-elected, the other two being new members of the board. No other change was made in the officers, except the election of Mr. M. Hutchinson as trustee.

In their 28th quarterly report, June 30th, the committee said their anticipations had not been realised that quarter. They had hoped to see a much greater increase in the receipts, so that they could have paid a dividend higher than that of the previous quarter, but in that, their cherished hope, they had been disappointed. There seemed to be slight progress-making, however, the sales being £2,230, and the dividend as in March, 1s. 3d. to members and a 1s. to non-members. The members' claims were £2,227 and the profit £140. Members, non-members, and friends were earnestly appealed to, to assist in endeavouring to carry out and develop the great principles of co-operation. The accounts were signed by I. Bardsley and T. Hodson, auditors.

The 29th report was very brief, consisting of just three lines of print. The committee took pleasure in stating that the society was in a prosperous condition, and the dividend to members was 1d. more—

1s. 4d. The sales were nearly £300 more than those of the preceding quarter, a very good increase for a September quarter over June, and £17 was devoted to the writing down of fixed stock.

At this time four days were allowed the staff as annual holidays.

The committee did just go into detail. Not only did they buy butter, flour, potatoes, &c., interviewing merchants or their representatives at committee meetings, but they issued to the shopmen a list of names of the committee, and any member with a complaint was referred to them. They passed a resolution the same year that a daily paper be bought for the use of the society; a resolution a few pages further on is that a ton of cheese be bought. One of their number was appointed to buy bacon from members.

Early in the year the committee-room was let to a loan society at a 1s. per week summer months, and 1s. 6d. winter.

The committee, doubtless, had lively recollections of their reception at the members' meetings during the dark years, and in April, 1866, they agreed that Mr. John Bamford should take the chair at the annual meeting, and that if he were objected to, Mr. Swift should be proposed.

It appears, however, that no objection was raised. Times were improving, and so was the position of the society. On several occasions it was resolved at annual meetings that a good supper be provided for the committee; the position became still better, and the members showed their appreciation by voting two good suppers.

CO-OPERATION IN STALYBRIDGE.

On Saturday, November 24th, 1866, 650 members and friends of the society took tea at the Mechanics' Institute. After tea a meeting was held under the presidency of J. Sidebottom, Esq., mayor of the borough, and upon the platform were the committee and several other friends of co-operation. The chairman, in opening the proceedings, briefly thanked the committee for having invited him a second time to preside at one of their festive gatherings, and assured them he had learned with great satisfaction that their society was prospering, after the adverse circumstances they had met with during the panic.

The Rev. J. P. Hopps, on rising to address the meeting, was well received, and during the delivery of an admirable address was much cheered. He referred to the great principle of co-operation, which he believed in more than anything else, after the Gospel of which he was one of the ministers. He believed in co-operation—not because it might be paying good dividends, but because it was a principle destined to work out the salvation of the people. If the society which had brought them together that night had been paying no dividend at all, he should still have had as firm a faith in the principles as if a large dividend had been paid. Failures did not make against the principles, for they were often the result of some bungling, which would be overcome as the principles were better understood. All good principles had been bungled over in their infancy, and great sciences were once great dreams, and, to some people's minds, great fallacies. They were now, however, acknowledged as great truths, and it would be the same with the principles of co-operation. The greater the principle, the longer it took to develop it. Co-operation was not a new thing; it had been often tried, and had often failed, but the failures had only tended to make it better understood, and would make it firmer in the end. He would not care much for co-operation if it was to end in a shop, and the occasional paying of a dividend, for if that had been all it was capable of doing, he would never leave his home on a Saturday night to advocate its principles. The speaker laid it down as a principle that "We must seek the good of every one in the good of all," and then argued that the man or woman who had not mastered that great principle of co-operation was not a co-operator. He next glanced at some of the advantages of co-operation to the members of a society, and said that although persons might join from purely selfish motives, beneficial results would follow. One important advantage was that of buying with ready money, for a working man who traded at a shop with a book was always behind, inasmuch as his wages were mortgaged. Such a man when he received his wages, could not close his hand upon them and say "These are mine." He related an incident of a reverend gentleman borrowing 5s. of a deacon just before he mounted the pulpit stairs to preach. After the sermon the money was returned to the deacon, to his evident surprise, who naturally inquired of the minister what he wanted it for, when the latter replied that he was able to preach a better sermon with money in his pocket. Mr. Hopps contended that it was the same with working men, and if they could carry their wages in their pockets until the following pay day they would work all the better for it. He would like to meet the working men of Stalybridge in public meeting some evening and tell them what he thought about co-operation, for he believed he could see in it a solution of all the difficulties that continually sprang up between masters and men, between capital and labour. Sometime ago he happened to be without a gardener, so he set to work himself, and he felt a far greater pleasure in looking on what had been grown under his own hand-labour, than he did in looking at what other people had grown for him. No turnips smelled so sweet to him as those he had worked for, while his potatoes, which were half bad, were to him the best in the parish, and all because he had laboured for them himself. He concluded his address by remarking that the dream he cherished was that the co-operative principle would hasten the time when masters and men would seek each other's welfare and happiness by seeking the good of everyone in the good of all.

Mr. Ridgway said the dream of Mr. Hopps was in the right direction, for if ever the great problem of capital and labour were solved it would be by the principles of co-operation.

The Rev. J. R. Stephens, in the course of his address said, "It is very good of you to ask me to take tea with you to-night. I have been at almost every kind of meeting, made up for the most part of the hand-workers in the trades of England, at which their leaders have had anything to say which they believed would tend to raise the low, strengthen the weak, and unite the broken-up and wide-scattered members of their order. But this is the first time I ever had the privilege of being present at a festive gathering of those who seek, by means of what they call co-operation, to break the bondage of the men who earn wages for doing another man's work, by teaching them how easy it is by their joint action of numbers, to pass into the charmed circle of the middle, money-making classes of their fellow-countrymen. Even in the undertaking in which you are most of you interested, this Stalybridge Good Intent Industrial Society, you have already found that your sphere of action is a limited one. You once had over a thousand members, and now have but six hundred; you once had four or five stores; you now have but one. You have been driven to admit that you are nothing but a simple joint stock company, and that your business must be managed just as private firms manage theirs. You have run risks, and have had serious losses. You now see that you did not make due allowance for the friction of your machinery. Nay, there was one period in your short history, when you were only saved from entire shipwreck by the persistent efforts of one or two individuals. You deserve success, and I hope you will achieve it. My sympathies are always with efforts of this description, because I know that those who make them are amongst the most meritorious of their class. They are men who would either do away with selfishness, or make selfishness an instrument of good to others. Your right to co-operate in trade rests on the same ground as that of any single individual to trade on his own private account. I think the peculiar characteristic of your co-partnery gives you an opportunity of fostering habits of thoughtfulness and frugality in those who were aforetimes improvident and wasteful, and you have so far conferred a great benefit on society. It is one of the serious drawbacks of our crowded towns that the individual is lost in the masses. Associations, therefore, of every kind which have a praiseworthy object in view ought by all means to be encouraged. There are some hundreds of you here to-night, and each one of you seems to know many of those around him, and you are evidently happy in each other's company. Good fellowship, leading to the interchange of kind acts one towards another, is of more value than the mere profit you derive as shareholders in the concern.

The Mayor, in returning thanks, said his ideas of co-operation had been enlightened by the addresses he had heard during the evening. It had been stated to be in its infancy, but if so, as it grew up and strengthened it would be productive of great benefit.

The remainder of the evening was devoted to music and dancing.

In January, 1867, the society's pound shares were bought at 17s., an advance of 3s. per share since May 1865. In April, 1867, they were at par. There was offered and accepted 19s. in 1869, but in 1870 they were once more 20s.

In the records of March, 1867, there is a reference to the Order of Druids, the Druids' tea party committee being allowed a dividend of 1s. per £ of their purchases.

The shopmen were paid partly by bonus. The

minutes read "that the servants be paid 2¼ per cent for conducting the business." Whether the bonus system or some other matter formed the bone of contention is not clear; whatever the cause, the men did not for some time agree. They even became somewhat destructive, and were mulcted in various sums. On one occasion 5s. 6d. was deducted from the commission or bonus for damage to a treacle puncheon. On another, 10s., one-half the loss by a base sovereign taken over the counter, was refunded from the bonus. A patent coin detector was ordered from Mr. Sykes, and the shopmen were afterwards held responsible for all base coins passed by them. The secretary was requested to quell any disturbance that might arise amongst the men, and two of the committee were sent to warn them against quarrelling.

The committee's report in March, 1867, was—" In presenting this report we are gratified in saying that the society continues to prosper. The dividend will be 1s. 6d. in the £ for members and 1s. for non-members."

The sales were £3,559, nearly double those of the corresponding quarter two years before. Membeis' share claims were £2,222; they had varied only from that to £2,431 since 1863. The rules provided that a member in distress could withdraw any sum he might have in the funds of the society above £2, at the discretion of the committee, and that discretion had been exercised in the direction of suspending the withdrawal of shares during those years of struggle.

From this point the business continued to grow. There were but the two departments, grocery and drapery, but sales were increasing. In June, 1867, it was arranged that members should be paid dividend on men's and boys' clothing purchased from Mr. J. D. Smith, tailor, &c., 126 and 128, Stamford Street, Ashton, Mr. Smith paying the society a commission. On November 23rd, 1868, Mr. John Dyson, tailor, Melbourne Street, Stalybridge, submitted an offer. Messrs. Unsworth and Ashworth were deputed to wait upon Mr. Dyson for the purpose of making terms, and Mr. Dyson's name was announced along with Mr. Smith's in the next report. From the amount received as commission it is estimated that after a year under this arrangement the tailoring trade averaged a little more than a suit per week.

Many years before this there had been general conferences of societies all over the country. They were discontinued for some years, but the northern societies held conferences in various places on Good Friday, under the "Conference Committee of the Lancashire and Yorkshire Co-operative Societies." In 1867 the conference was held in Manchester, and Mr. John Thorp was appointed to represent Stalybridge Society there. The following year Mr. Peter Unsworth was the Stalybridge delegate, and the conference was held at Halifax. Another year later, 1869, the general conferences were re-established, owing in a great measure to the efforts of Mr. E. O. Greening. A guarantee fund for the expenses of the experiment was formed, and Mr. William Pare, one of the oldest disciples of Robert Owen, was honorary secretary. The Stalybridge Society made a contribution of a farthing per member. From that date to the present

CO-OPERATION IN STALYBRIDGE. 133

time the gathering has been known as the Annual Congress. Mr. Pare had been Registrar of births, marriages, and deaths, in Birmingham, but was compelled to resign the office when it became known to the Bishop of Exeter that he sympathised with Mr. Owen's views.

It has been said by a speaker at one of our gatherings in Stalybridge that co-operative work did not require kid gloves in those days, and certainly such articles would have been out of place in some of the work undertaken by our predecessors. One who had been on the committee not long before undertook to empty the ashes. The man was evidently a handy sort of fellow, for later on he arranged to personally point the warehouse wall.

The *Ashton-under-Lyne Reporter* of October 17th, 1868, gives the following account of the vicissitudes through which the society had passed, and of the annual party :—

> Few co-operative societies in the country ever went through such a chequered career as the Stalybridge Good Intent Industrial Co-operative Society. Formed some nine years ago, when work was plentiful and wages good, it soon consisted of thousands of members. They seemed to be imbued with the opinion that the society would soon be able to do all the business in the town, and stores were opened in two streets, and branches formed at Millbrook, Hurst, and Waterloo. The cry was for more members and still further extension, but at last the policy proved to be a dangerous one.
>
> Suspicions sprang up, members left, branches cut their connections, quarrels ensued, annual meetings were productive of scenes of an unpleasant character, shares depreciated, and everything seemed to be going to the dogs, when a band of true co-operators arose and cried

134 CO-OPERATION IN STALYBRIDGE.

for retrenchment, and after a great fight the rules were amended. Shops were reduced, property bought, the business was conducted in a more business-like manner, and instead of shares being offered in the lump at eight and ten shillings each, they cannot be bought by the public under £1. 1s. This is a great and beneficial change, and great praise is due to the men who have brought it about.

On Saturday last (October 10th) the annual tea party was held in the Mechanics' Institution, when over 600 persons were present, and a very social tea was enjoyed. The materials were supplied from the stores in Grosvenor Street, and it is the barest record of a simple fact to say that they reflected the highest credit on the manager. After tea, Mr. John Ridgway occupied the chair, and an excellent quadrille band was in attendance. The proceedings commenced by Mr. Joseph Greenwood, the secretary, reading the thirty-seventh quarterly report, from which the following is taken:—" The dividend to the members for the quarter is 1s. 8d. in the £, and to non-members 1s. 3d. All stores close on Mondays and Wednesdays at 8 p.m., Tuesdays at 2 p.m., Thursdays, Fridays, and Saturdays, 9 p.m. Cash received for groceries during the quarter, £3,369. 9s. 2d.; drapery, £237. 18s. 5d. Among the disbursements were—Groceries, £3,271. 1s. 1d.; drapery, £161. 19s. 11d.; wages, £81. 3s.; shares purchased, £10. 1s. 6d.; interest and dividend, £284. 11s. 6d. The liabilities were—Members' claims, £1,915. 17s. 8d.; interest, £48; bills owing, £199. 3s. 10d.; balance profit, £282. 9s. 3d.; making a total of £2,489. 0s. 10d. The assets were—Cash in hand, £170. 2s. 7d.; goods in stock, £1,639. 11s. 8d.; fixed stock, £120; property, £513; invested in Rochdale Corn Mill Society, £29. 6s. 7d.

The Board of Management consisted of Messrs. Wm. Harrison, John Bamford, Matthew Hutchison, John Hampshire, Marshall Ashworth, John Thorpe, Peter Unsworth, Joseph Kay, Robert Bullock, George Woodhead, John Lawton, Joseph Cottrell.

At the end of 1868 a quarter's sales, for the first time since the days of the cotton panic, topped £4,000. Mr. James Lawton, who had followed Mr. Johanan Booth as treasurer in 1862, retired, and a vote of thanks to him was passed. He was succeeded by Mr. John Ridgway. There was passed through Mr. Ridgway's hands, December quarter, 1868, £4,222 for goods sold.

CHAPTER IX.

1869 TO 1874—LARGE GATHERING OF MEMBERS AND FRIENDS
—OTHER TAILORING AGENCIES—MAKING KNOWN THE
"CO-OPERATIVE NEWS"—MR. GREENWOOD RETIRES—
MR. P. H. ROBINSON AND MR. F. R. BEELEY APPOINTED—
MISS HAMPSHIRE RETIRES—MISS WOOLLEY APPOINTED
—THE SOCIETY BECOMES A MEMBER OF THE CO-OPERATIVE
WHOLESALE SOCIETY.

ON Saturday evening, October 30th, 1869, members and friends to the number of 800 held their annual tea party in the Mechanics' Institute. Mr. John Bamford was called upon to preside. He said he knew some of the young people had come purposely to dance, but he was sure the addresses which would be delivered would be both edifying and instructive.

Mr. Greenwood urged the members to do their best to induce their friends to join; it was not a thing to be lightly passed over, he said. They ought not to rest satisfied with becoming members themselves, they should tell their neighbours, like women tell secrets, and then it would be certain to spread. He concluded by showing that the society was in a fair way to becoming very prosperous, notwithstanding the many drawbacks.

Mr. Thomas Hodson, one of the auditors, said he had been an auditor for three or four years, and had had full liberty to pry into their business, and from what he knew of their affairs, and from what he knew of their officers, he was sure that all concerned were doing their best for the welfare of the society. He complimented them on having such a manager ; he was not hasty, neither was he slow, and he could truly say that he got through a great deal of work. To have a good manager was a great thing, for as he worked, so worked others—they all imitated him. He heard a great deal about dividends from other towns, and he thought they ought not to rest satisfied until they had gained a firm footing for themselves. He thought they had accomplished great things, but he advised them to curtail the expenses, and not to allow any wrong to go on for a moment. He trusted their society would still prosper, and become a great and useful institution.

Mr. J. Ridgway was then called upon to say a few words to the ladies. On former occasions he had spoken about them, but he had received a hint that he must not say much about the faults of the ladies. He believed that if the stores had to depend solely upon the gentlemen they would soon go wrong. It was the ladies who did the buying, and the prosperity of the store was mainly owing to their influence. He showed the evil influence which drink had upon the people, and also the great change which would take place were that money spent in clothing and food ; how it would make families happier, and their members more useful in society. He thought their society could now be placed among the great institutions of the town, and if they could keep the ladies on their side they would prosper.

Mr. Hutchison said that if there were more co-operative stores there would be less work for the mayor and magistrates to do on Monday mornings. He reverted to a time when the society was in difficulties. At that time they left to others what they ought to have done themselves, but he was glad to state that the shares were now worth twenty shillings in the £, and if they went on as they were doing they would soon be worth twenty-five shillings.

The Shepherds' Band, which had been engaged to lead the dancing, at that moment arrived in front of the institution, and the room was cleared. The rest of the evening was spent in dancing, or listening to the music by the band. Mr. J. Duffy acted as master of ceremonies.

Mr. Marcroft said he had paid a visit to the store that day, and he was happy to find that they were in a satisfactory state, and that the society was not troubled with a great fixed stock. The best and safest means of reducing their working expenses was to increase the quantity of goods sold. If it happened that they saw flour at another shop marked lower than at their own store, he would advise them to make a calculation, and he would guarantee that they would be as well served by themselves as at any other place. He said he had thought a great deal about co-operation, and was sure that if he had become a member of a co-operative store years before he did, he would then have been able to leave off working, and live at his ease. The speaker here said that in Stalybridge there was a great waste going on, they were using more gas than they had any need to. He would advise them to note how many shops there were in the borough, how many workshops, public-houses, &c., and then to calculate how many co-operative stores it would take to carry on the business done, and they would be surprised to find how much the borough would be the gainer by working on the co-operative principle. He would advise them to canvas for their co-operative store as they did for a councilman or member of Parliament, and to act charitably, as did the Great Reformer 1,800 years ago. He alluded to the troublous times of twenty-five years before, and stated that when they were told in Oldham that Ashton people were coming to commit depredations, the co-operators told the police they had no need to drive them back, for they—the co-operators—would do that; it was they who could say "This mill is ours, and we will protect it." He referred to Mr. James Smithies, one of the famous twenty-eight pioneers of Rochdale, and concluded amidst loud cheers.

On the 21st February, 1870, the committee accepted terms offered by Messrs. Killorn, tailors and drapers, George Street, Ashton, for the supplying of men's and boys' clothing to members, the society to receive a commission. Business was still done with Mr. J. D. Smith, of Ashton, and Mr. John Dyson, of Stalybridge, and it appears that for the quarter ended June, 1870, the society received commission on between £70 and £80 business from the three tailoring houses. The society's general dividend had, however, been creeping up ; it had reached 1s. 10d., and the commission paid by the tailors was considered too small. Hence it was resolved, April 25th, 1870, that the society cease to do any more tailors' business on the present commission. A month later it was arranged that the tailors should themselves pay the society's members 5 per cent on the business done.

The dividend was 2s. to members and 1s. 7d. to non-members in September, 1870, and in December quarter the sales were £5,469. For the first time since October, 1862, a reserve fund appeared in the accounts, June, 1870 ; it was £35 in June, and had increased to £55 in December.

On the 7th May, 1870, the Stalybridge baths were opened, and the society's shops were closed for the occasion from 2 to 6 o'clock.

There was an effort in 1871 to popularise the *Co-operative News*. Copies were sent to the Mechanics' Institution, the Conservative Rooms, and the Reform Rooms, and it was announced in the reports that the *News* could be obtained, price one penny weekly, from the check clerk.

It has been related how the employés were fined for damage done. On the other hand the committee appear to have been desirous of rewarding merit. In one instance in 1872 they passed the weighty resolution that W. R. be awarded a shilling for his alertness in detecting forged checks.

At a special meeting of the members held Thursday, 21st August, 1873, Mr. John Ridgway presiding, revised rules were adopted. They included a provision that no person who had a relative employed by

THE STAFF IN THE EARLY 'SEVENTIES.

F. R. BEELEY, S. McCALL, WM. LAWTON, GROCER, JOSEPH GREENWOOD, SECRETARY,
WM. RADCLIFFE, Check Boy, MISS HAMPSHIRE, DRAPERY MANAGER, JAMES LIVESEY, GROCER, P. H. ROBINSON, MANAGER.

the society should serve on the committee. This was altered some time later to "near" relative, and although a question has once at least arisen as to the definition of "near," it is thought that the provision is a wise one, tending toward avoidance of a difficulty, not unknown to other societies, in maintaining discipline where members of committees have sons or daughters employed.

It was in the year 1873 that Mr. Joseph Greenwood retired from the secretaryship. The annual meeting held May 1st tendered its warmest thanks for the able and straightforward manner in which he had discharged his duties. Miss Hampshire, who had charge of the drapery whilst Mr. Greenwood was secretary, said of him that there could not be a more conscientious man. It is said, too, that on retiring he expressed a hope that on no account would a presentation to him be made. That hope seems to have been characteristic of the man. He was for some time connected with another institution in the town, and when he retired the other members of the committee decided to recognise his services. A watch was bought and an inscription engraved upon it, and Mr. Greenwood was invited to meet his colleagues. He did so, but he declined the watch. It was known that he could not bear anything approaching ostentation, and the watch was placed in the care of Mr. Ridgway with a request that it should be handed over privately. It was offered on more than one occasion and the reply was that it would one day be accepted. Mr. Greenwood made certain inquiries, and then announced his willingness to accept the watch. Mr. Ridgway expressed his pleasure and handed it over. Mr. Greenwood took it with one hand, and paid the cost with the other.

Miss Hampshire (now Mrs. Worsley), as already related, had been in the drapery when the department was in Caroline Street, and went with it to Grosvenor Street. She was appointed drapery buyer in 1873. Interviewed in 1909, Mrs. Worsley said she was with the society ten years. The first week she was there £8 was taken. She had an offer from the Rochdale Pioneers Society, but decided not to leave home. She said that for some time it was uphill work at Stalybridge, but the £8 turnover was increased to £50. They would ask a member " What do you want for dividend this time ? " The answer was " A pair of blankets," or " a shawl " or whatever other article was most required, and sometimes when dividend week came round as much as £100 would be taken. The group comprising the entire staff in the early seventies is taken from a photograph now in the possession of Mrs. Worsley, and kindly lent for the purpose. It was taken by Mr. W. Emmett, and many members of the society obtained copies.

In April, 1873, an advertisement appeared in the *Co-operative News* for a competent person to act as secretary and buyer. Mr. Philip H. Robinson, who was described by Miss Hampshire as an ambitious young man, and who had been employed as shopman since 1866, was appointed to the position on the 21st April, in succession to Mr. Greenwood. Mr. J. H. Milligan, now Central grocery manager, was appointed as a boy to the drapery department the same year, and

remembers Mr. Robinson well. He says he never knew a smarter shopman.

Mr. F. R. Beeley, the present school board officer, was a contemporary of Mr. Robinson. Mr. Beeley was made head shopman on the 21st April, 1873, and was required to find bond for £50 a year later. On the 29th April, 1874, there was a rearrangement of the duties, and Mr. Beeley became manager and buyer, Mr. Robinson retaining the office of secretary. Mr. Beeley remained as manager until 1876, when Mr. J. Mellor came.

It was about the beginning of 1874 that Miss Hampshire left, and on the 18th February Miss Woolley (now Mrs. Mellor) was appointed by a sub-committee consisting of Messrs. Peter Unsworth, John Heap, and Allen Heppenstall. Miss Woolley had the management of drapery until June, 1887, and under her care the department experienced a more than three-fold growth. Her first year the drapery sales were £2,242; in her last they had increased to £7,012. Mr. Frank E. Maden, who commenced his business career with the society, followed Miss Woolley as drapery manager, and Miss J. B. Ellis was appointed to the department in July the same year.

The society became a member of the Co-operative Wholesale Society in 1874, a recommendation of the committee being adopted at the annual meeting held 8th April. The Rochdale Pioneers had had a wholesale department which had to a certain extent supplied the societies in Lancashire and Yorkshire, and the honour of being the founder of the Co-operative Wholesale Society belongs to Mr. Abraham Greenwood, of

Rochdale. The Rochdale Pioneers' store was started by a twopenny subscription ; the great Wholesale Society itself was actually set going by a contribution—not a subscription from week to week—of one farthing per member from societies which had agreed to become shareholders. The benefits were thus foretold by Mr. Greenwood, the founder—

1. Stores would be able to purchase more carefully and cheaply, by reaching the best markets.
2. Small stores would at once be placed in as good a position for selling the same quality and as cheaply as any first-rate shopkeeper.
3. All the stores having the benefit of the best markets, the dividends would be more equal ; and in the same way, the working expenses being reduced, the dividend would be greater.
4. Large stores could carry on their business with less capital, because they need only take from the Wholesale depôt what they required for immediate use.
5. Stores could get the services of a good buyer, since one experienced man could as easily buy for 150 stores as for one.

On the 11th August, 1863, the English Co-operative Wholesale Society was enrolled, and on the 14th March, 1864, business was commenced. Doubtless the co-operators of Stalybridge saw the advantages of membership of a concern which had a trade turnover, when they joined it, of nearly £2,000,000. Did they anticipate, we wonder, the present magnitude of the same

Wholesale Society? Commencing as stated with a farthing contribution, it has a grocery department employing 300 persons, a drapery with 200 employed, corn mills with a greater output than those of any other millers in the country, biscuit works employing 500, preserve works 600, tailoring factory 500, boot factories between 3,000 and 4,000, soap works turning out hundreds of tons of soap per week, iron works, weaving shed, and many other departments employing together more than 18,000 people, with a trade turnover of £25,000,000 and a bank turnover of £100,000,000 a year, a reserve fund approaching half a million, and in such a position that it can make donations of thousands of pounds at a time for charitable purposes.

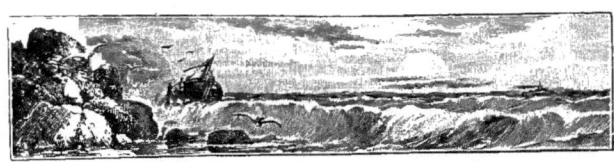

CHAPTER X.

1874 TO 1880—CENTRAL PREMISES EXTENSION—MR. SETH CHARLESWORTH, SECRETARY—COPPER POUND CHECKS—MR. J. MELLOR APPOINTED MANAGER—HIGH STREET BRANCH OPENED—STEAM POWER—CORN MILL SHARES—RESERVE FUND £1,000—COMMITTEE AND STAFF TOGETHER AT TEA—EXISTING MILLBROOK BRANCH OPENED—QUARTERLY CONFERENCE ENTERTAINED—LOAN ACCOUNT—A START IN THE BOOT TRADE—COFFEE ROASTING—EXCURSIONS.

THE next step forward was an extension of the Central premises. Negotiations had been proceeding since December, 1872, until on the 17th April, 1874, the committee were empowered by a special meeting of members to purchase two blocks of buildings in Back Grosvenor Street, consisting of eleven cottages, and to proceed with an extension to the rear of the Grosvenor Street shop. Two or three years before, the building and fixtures were valued at £400; the cottages were bought for £766, and the whole, including shops and houses, was valued in the balance sheet of December, 1874, at £766. Thus the cost of the original Grosvenor Street shop had been entirely

CO-OPERATION IN STALYBRIDGE. 153

written off, and the society was well prepared for expenditure on alterations and new premises.

Mr. James Lawton was retained as architect, and in July, 1875, Mr. Levi Warrington's tender for new buildings and alterations to existing buildings was accepted. The contract provided for the building complete and finishing of a certain shop, offices, cellars, store rooms, hoist, and other buildings on land and premises adjoining and contiguous to Grosvenor Street and Back Grosvenor Street. Whilst building operations were going on, the shop, No. 10, Grosvenor Street, was rented, and the drapery business was conducted entirely there. It is not the present (1909) drapery building that is here referred to. It was in 1884 that the existing drapery and boot premises were erected, and in 1905 that the drapery front was rebuilt.

In November, 1875, the entrance fee and contribution to shares were fixed at what they are now, 1s. the former, and 2s. 6d. per quarter the latter until two shares are paid up.

Messrs. John Jackson and John Heap were auditors, and Mr. Seth Charlesworth secretary. Many will remember Mr. Charlesworth, who had but one arm, and that his left. The right had been amputated as the result of a knock. He was a clerk with Mossley Society prior to coming to Stalybridge, and was appointed secretary here on the 29th October, 1874. Mr. J. R. Jackson succeeded him in 1880.

The prices of some commodities were at this time, 1874, much higher than at present. Flour, for instance, was selling at 2s. 1d. a dozen. Not very long before that lump sugar was 6½d. per lb., and the profit was so precarious that purchases of sugar were not subject to dividend. This year, 1874, the committee resolved that "Checks be given on sugar, but that no person be served with more than is required," the intention being, probably, to prevent a run on the article by speculative people.

It appears from the accounts of the time that there was no longer any restriction on the withdrawal of shares, but the cash received from members on account of shares was largely in excess of the withdrawals.

In March, 1876, it was announced that arrangements had been made for the purchase of a sufficient supply of copper pound checks, to take the place of the paper pound checks then in use. The new checks were issued the following quarter, and for the purpose of distinction differed in shape successive quarters.

In June, 1876, the Back Grosvenor Street extension was nearing completion, and the architect prepared plans for an alteration of the old shop. The front was completely renovated by Messrs. William Storrs and Sons, and in March, 1877, the building was completed, the grocery department occupying the front, and drapery being removed to the rear.

It was on the 1st September, 1876, that Mr. J. Mellor was appointed manager. He came from the Rochdale Pioneers' Society, as did Mr. J. B. Mason, our present manager. When Mr. Mellor came there were but grocery and drapery, and a year's sales amounted to £34,134. He saw boots, tailoring, butchering, and coal departments opened, and retired in April, 1895, when a year's sales totalled £56,303. He was present, hale and hearty at one, at least, of the Jubilee gatherings in 1909.

No. 1 Branch — High Street

CO-OPERATION IN STALYBRIDGE. 159

On October 11th, 1876, the large room of the Town Hall was hired for the half-yearly meeting.

Many will remember the old office, with its outer office used for paying dividend and taking in checks, at the top of the staircase leading from the present Central grocery. The dividend and check office, as it was known, was simply a space outside the general office enclosed by panelled woodwork open at the top. It appears that more than one means of obtaining access had been adopted, and the committee found it necessary to pass a resolution that an extra key to the dividend and check office be provided, and that no one be allowed to climb over the top.

On the 7th May, 1877, three shops and four cottages in High Street, Stalybridge, were bought at the Commercial Inn; on the 18th June the assignment of the property was sealed, and at once preparations for opening a branch store were made. Mr. Fred Gee was placed in charge of the branch September 3rd, and Mr. Edward Hassall went with him.

Inquiries as to steam power had been instituted, and on the 15th October, 1877, it was decided that an engine and boiler be purchased from Messrs. Goodbrand and Holland, of Manchester.

At the end of 1877 the committee congratulated the members on the continued success of the society. Their reports for several quarters had been without a doleful note; now they were giving expression to a feeling of confidence that the results would prove satisfactory to all concerned. The quarterly sales for the first time since pre-panic days ran well into five figures, being £10,059 for the thirteen weeks ended

September 29th, and £10,056 for the eleven weeks ended December 15th, averages of £773 and £914 per week respectively. There were still only grocery and drapery, but High Street Branch, opened in September, had taken in fourteen weeks £2,305, an average of £164 a week. The sales at the Central grocery department alone averaged no less than £686 per week for the six months ended December 15th, and the drapery average was £55 per week. The dividend was 2s. 6d., and there were substantial amounts devoted to the reduction of buildings and fixtures, the entire balance of the Back Grosvenor Street cottages being written off. The committee would be feeling their way toward a demolition which took place later, the cottages being replaced by shops. There was also a first grant from the profits of £10 for an education fund. There were 1,341 members, an increase of 333 during the year, and their shares totalled £7,845. The society's holding in shares of the Wholesale Society had increased to £272 ; in Star Corn Mill shares there was £202 ; and in Rochdale Corn Mill shares £94.

In disposing of the profits, June, 1878, a sum of £43 was added to the reserve fund, making £1,000 exactly.

The committee and employés met at tea in the society's meeting-room on Friday evening, January 3rd, 1879. Mr. John Heap, of the committee, took the chair. Messrs. Heppenstall and Betts rendered the instrumental part of the programme, and songs were given by Messrs. Samuel Whitehead, John Hague, and James Hague (who had been engaged for the occasion), by John Heap, Maria Fogarty, and others.

No. 2 Branch.—Millbrook.

Mr. Wm. Hall gave a very timely recitation, entitled "A Happy New Year to Yo' O'," and John Pinder whistled the "Eclipse Polka," with variations.

On the 28th February, 1879, the present Millbrook Branch was opened. Prior to that there were arrangements for the delivery by cart of goods at Millbrook; in 1872 it was once a fortnight only. The proposal to erect a branch there was accepted at an adjourned meeting of members held 24th October, 1877, Mr. John Swan being the mover and Mr. Samuel Wallwork the seconder. There was some opposition, an amendment being moved and seconded that no branch store be established outside the borough. Early in 1878 negotiations with the steward to the Earl of Stamford and Warrington were concluded, and the plot of land between the church school and Hartley's property taken, Messrs. John Buckley and William Hall meeting the steward. Mr. James Lawton, the architect, prepared plans for a store and eight houses, and builders' work was commenced about June, 1878. Mr. Robert Wilkinson was the builder, and the contract price was £2,100. Later Messrs. Broadbent and Shaw's tender for counters, shelves, and bins, £65, was accepted, and Messrs. Askew Dawson and Co. undertook the gasfitting. In December, 1878, the houses were announced ready for tenants, and the rents fixed. The decoration of the houses was let to Messrs. Smith and Stansfield in the July following. Mr. James Broadbent took charge as branch manager. From the start the Millbrook members seemed proud of their shop and it did well. From the opening day, February 28th, to the end of the quarter, March 19th, the sales were £242, and for the first complete quarter £1,119.

164   CO-OPERATION IN STALYBRIDGE.

As early as 1879 Millbrook Fair is referred to, a subscription being paid in May of that year.

On the 15th March, 1879, the members celebrated, at the house of Mr. Moses Slater, Hare and Hounds Inn, Millbrook, the opening of the branch. Upwards of 160 persons sat down to tea. The Mossley Brass Band was present, under the leadership of Mr. Squire Wrigley, and Mr. Wm. Hall, ex-president of the society, took the chair. Mr. Thomas Moss, in a few remarks, said if the members would rally round their new store he was sure it would prosper. There were songs by Mr. John Hague, Mr. H. Ingham, and Mr. John Lawton, the last-named giving, by desire, "Millbrook Band;" and Mr. James Wood, the celebrated trombone player, gave a solo, "Death of Nelson." Mr. Hall moved and Mr. Ben Lee seconded a vote of thanks to Mr. and Mrs. Slater.

The quarterly conference of the district was invited to Stalybridge in 1879. The Oddfellows' Hall was hired for the occasion, provision for an attendance of 120 persons made, and Mr. John Ridgway was asked to preside. The arrangements were placed in the hands of Mr. Samuel Sidebottom and Mr. John Street, and invitations were sent to the auditors, Messrs. John Jackson and John Heap, Mr. Forbes of the *Reporter*, Mr. Foreman of the *Standard*, and to the committees, secretaries, and treasurers of Ashton, Uppermill, and Mossley societies.

For many years a loan account was open. In 1869 sums of £1 to £50 at a time, and £300 in all were received from individual members, and the rate of interest was as high as 5 per cent. Members were

steadily increasing their shares, however, and loan-holders were gradually paid out. In 1877 the rate of interest on loans was reduced to 4 per cent, and in 1880 the account was closed. Indeed capital was so plentiful that some three years later, when there was a proposal that man and wife or other member of the family should be allowed to open separate accounts, it was promptly vetoed, and the year following that the share account was closed to all but incoming members.

A start in the boot trade was made in April, 1879. It was announced that a large assortment of boots and shoes manufactured by the Co-operative Wholesale Society at Leicester, was held in the drapery department. About the same time coffee-roasting on the premises was announced. The price, ground or unground, was 1s. 8d. per pound. Very large orders for this article were given, as much as five tons at a time of new East India coffee being bought.

In 1880 and for several years there were excursions to Blackpool and Liverpool on Stalybridge Wakes Tuesdays, and they were very popular, large numbers of people joining them. The arrangements were largely in the hands of Mr. Burgess, of the London and North-Western Company, and were admirably carried out.

CHAPTER XI.

1881 TO 1884—STALYBRIDGE COTTON MILL SHARES—NO. 3 BRANCH OPENED—A THREE-SHILLINGS DIVIDEND—£50,000 SALES—THOMAS HUGHES TESTIMONIAL—EXTENSION OF HIGH STREET BRANCH—MANCHESTER ROYAL EYE HOSPITAL—HEBDEN BRIDGE FUSTIAN SOCIETY SHARES—CROOKBOTTOM MANUFACTURING COMPANY SHARES—EXTENSION, BACK GROSVENOR STREET—LARGE GATHERING, 1884—FIRST ADVANCE ON HOUSE PROPERTY—HUDDERSFIELD ROAD BRANCH OPENED—COAL TRADE COMMENCED.

THERE appears to have been a long discussion at the quarterly meeting held July 6th, 1881, of a proposal to take up shares of the Stalybridge Cotton Mill Company. There was a motion that 200 shares be taken, an amendment that only 100 be taken, and a rider that it be 400. Tellers were appointed, and it was found that 45 members voted for 400 shares, 2 members for 100 shares, and 15 members for 200 shares. Four hundred shares were taken up and Mr. John Heap was appointed to represent the society at the company's meetings until the date of the next annual meeting of members. The shares are still held.

No. 3 Branch.—Mount Pleasant.

There was before the quarterly meeting held January 5th, 1881, a proposal for a branch store " on the Lancashire side of the borough." At least three or four different properties were inspected between that date and May, when a special meeting of members empowered the committee to purchase Mr. Simpson's property at Mount Pleasant. There were 35 votes for and 2 against. In June, 1881, Mr. James Lawton's plans were adopted. The tenders of Messrs. Garside, Barnes and Co. for the building, and Messrs. Shaw and Cuzner for counter and shelving, were accepted. Messrs. John Buckley, F. B. Wilde, John Shaw, and William Hall were appointed a Building Committee. Mr. Edward Hassall was appointed manager of the new branch, No. 3, and it was opened about April, 1882, a party in commemoration of the opening being held on Saturday the 22nd, in the Mechanics' Institution. About 900 sat down to tea. After tea the chair was occupied by Mr. F. B. Wilde, president. He said he hoped the opening of Mount Pleasant Branch, which they were met to celebrate, would be an auspicious one. If there was one thing more gratifying than another in connection with that festival, it was the position of the society, which had been entirely under the control of working men. They were there that night to show what working men could do, by the help of the ladies. Co-operation was slowly but surely making progress, especially in Stalybridge, not only in distribution, but in production too, and as a proof of it he might refer them to the partially-built mill of which they were one of the largest shareholders. Co-operation had helped to elevate the members, and the ready-cash system taught them the value of money, and made them more thrifty and industrious, better thinking men and women. The society had become a great undertaking, and was in a prosperous position, thanks to the efforts of the past committee and others who had done so much to overcome the many trials and difficulties. With reference to the Mount Pleasant Branch the committee had spared neither time nor trouble to bring it to a successful issue. It had so far been a thorough success, and the building was a credit to the society and an ornament to the town. (Cheers.) The report of Mr. J. R. Jackson, secretary, was presented, and there was an entertainment by Mr. J. H. Greenwood, of Manchester, Messrs. Butterworth and Holland, and others. There was an assembly for dancing in the Oddfellows' Hall which was largely attended.

From the opening to June 14th, the end of the quarter, £1,764 was taken over the counters of the new branch. As the Central sales were barely £1,000 down from the corresponding quarter of the year before, and the other branches had only small increases, it may be assumed that the opening of the new branch had the effect of increasing the turnover by £700.

The *Reporter*, commenting April 29th, 1882, said that the Co-operative Society appeared to have passed through another successful year, having received £47,509, giving a weekly average of £913. The report was satisfactory at a glance, and must have been a source of gratification to the members, who were described as the thriftiest of the inhabitants of the borough.

There was another effort this year to increase the sale of the *Co-operative News*. The weekly order was increased and it was sold at half-price, as at present.

The profit available for dividend had been creeping up, although there were some set-backs. The dividend had been 2s. 9d., then back to 2s. 6d. for one quarter, 2s. 9d. for two quarters, 2s. 10d., 2s. 9d., 2s. 9d., 2s. 10d., 2s. 11d., until in June, 1882, the committee found themselves in a position to declare a dividend of 3s., with a surplus of £56, which was disposed of by writing down properties and adding to the reserve fund. At the end of 1882 the members numbered more than 2,000, and the sales for the first time exceeded £50,000.

At a quarterly meeting held January 3rd, 1883, a donation of £10 to a fund for a testimonial to Thomas Hughes, Q.C., was passed. As Professor Adamson, of Owen's College, said, when presiding at a lecture on "The History and Objects of Co-operation," by Mr. Hughes, in Manchester, April, 1878, Mr. Hughes was recognised as one of the foremost of those who had devoted themselves to the noble task of social improvement. In the lecture referred to Mr. Hughes spoke of himself as a co-operator, and expressed a hope that the principles of association adopted at the first conference in 1852, and acknowledged ever since by the societies, would be carried out. He was no believer, he said, in millenniums ; he had no faith in any good coming to any class or to any man without much hard work, and much self-denial. But this much he was prepared to say, that to a certain extent co-operation had already organised consumption, and to some extent production also, for at least 3,000,000 of English citizens. That meant, he said, that the scramble of life, the struggle for existence, had been made easier for all those English folk, and all who were the least aware what that struggle implied would ask for no nobler testimony of work for any movement. All he would ask was why, what had been done in 25 years, imperfectly, no doubt for 3,000,000, should not, in 50 years, be done far more perfectly for 10,000,000. What Mr. Hughes thought might be, has been achieved for that number of people. He went on to suggest that what might be done for 10,000,000 might be done in time for a nation. The very thought of a nation, he continued, whose industry was organised on co-operative principles filled the mind with visions of a time when the great problem of the nineteenth century would be solved, and the union between labour and capital stand out as a fact, and not a dream. Mr. Hughes was also joint editor with Mr. E. V. Neale, then general secretary to the Co-operative Union, of the admirable " Manual for Co-operators," prepared at the request of the Co-operative Congress held at Gloucester in 1879, and published for the Co-operative Union.

Business at High Street Branch had quite outgrown the premises, and in March, 1883, a plan for its extension, by Mr. James Lawton, was accepted. The contract for builders' work was let to Mr. H. France, Messrs. R. Dawson and Company's tender for heating by hot water was accepted, and Messrs. Garside,

Barnes and Company did the paving. There is here another reminder of the methods of former days in grocery, when large treacle cisterns filled from an upper floor were the rule. Such cisterns were adopted at a cost of considerably over £20 for use at the branch.

It was on the 3rd January, 1883, that the members decided to subscribe annually to an institution that has been of inestimable service to sufferers over a very wide area, the Manchester Royal Eye Hospital. Mr. J. B. W. Buckley moved, and Mr. George Britain seconded, the present subscription.

In the following month the society became a shareholder of the Hebden Bridge Fustian Manufacturing Society Limited.

It was also in that year, at a special meeting of the members held on the 15th May, that it was decided to take up 400 shares in the Crookbottom Manufacturing Company. Mr. J. H. Tyson was the mover, and Mr. George Britain the seconder. There was an amendment moved by Mr. Wm. Booth, and seconded by Mr. Joshua Shaw, that no shares be taken up. Some three years later a further sum of £500 was advanced as a loan. The engines were started February 14th, 1885, but the concern did not prosper. For several years a policy of writing down was followed, until in June, 1891, the shares, which had been fully paid (£2,000) were taken in the accounts at £1,650. That quarter the end came and the balance of £1,650, together with the amount of the loan, £500, was taken from the reserve fund. Later there was a dividend of £72. 18s. 4d. received from the liquidators, the net result being that the reserve fund was depleted to the extent of £2,078, from £2,365 to £287. Thus the total loss to the society would be £2,427.

Mr. James Lawton, the architect, was requested in November, 1883, to prepare plans and specification for the alteration of Back Grosvenor Street premises, and on the 2nd January, 1884, the quarterly meeting of members gave the committee power to proceed with the extension. Tenders were invited, and that of Messrs. Shaw, Cuzner and Co. for builders' work was accepted in March. Other work such as fixtures for office, boot department, and millinery was undertaken by Mr. A. Chorlton; additional seats for the meeting-room, the enlargement of which would be included in the builders' contract, were obtained from Mr. J. Jefferson; and the heating of the premises was placed in the hands of Mr. John Swain, of Hyde. The extension here referred to would include the present boot department, and the front portion of the present drapery, but not the rear portion of drapery, which was built some six years later, a stable being taken down to make space for it. The drapery front was still further improved in 1905.

A tea party and entertainment was held in the Mechanics' Institution, February 23rd, 1884. The number of people who partook of tea was considerably over 1,000, the hall being crowded. There was a quartette composed of Miss Janet Smith (soprano) and Miss Maud Yates (contralto) of the Manchester concerts, with Mr. Charles Moody (tenor) and Mr. Joseph Cartlidge (bass) of Stalybridge. Besides this, the talented comedy artistes, known as " The Merrions "' (Will, Harry, and Fred) appeared in their mirthful, musical entertainment, and Miss Lilian Roberts, the clever young reciter of Stalybridge, also contributed to the enjoyment of the evening. Mr. Enos Andrew was the accompanist, and Mr. F. B. Wilde occupied the chair. At the Oddfellows' Hall a dance was held, Mr. Lockwood's string band supplying the music. At this meeting also the attendance was very large, and it was suggested that the gathering should be made an annual one. The annual report of the secretary, Mr. J. R. Jackson, showed that during 1883 the receipts had been higher, and the profits larger, than in any year of the society's history, and that the members had been steadily increasing in number year by year. During the recent strike, he said, there was only £27. 11s. 6d. withdrawn, and during dividend week, just at the termination of the strike, there was credited to members' capital dividend and interest amounting to £516. The year's sales were £58,416, an increase of £6,576, and nearly £12,000 more than two years before. The dividend paid or credited, at 3s. per £, was £8,744, and properties had been reduced and the reserve fund added to. The latter amounted to £1,820.

The entertainment consisted of popular songs by the artistes named, all of whom were frequently applauded. The elocutionary abilities of Miss Lilian Roberts were well known, and will still be remembered by many. In the newspaper account of the time it is stated that she secured the favour of the large audience from the commencement. The performances of the Merrions were of an exceedingly clever and humorous character, and kept the audience in continual laughter.

The first advance to a member with house property for security was made June, 1884.

Huddersfield Road Branch was opened about the end of June, 1884. There was an application for a branch in September, 1882, from the members in the district, and on the 18th October of that year a special meeting of members was held. Mr. John Lees moved, and Mr. John Hopwood seconded—"That a branch store for Huddersfield Road district be established." There was an amendment that there be no branch store there. The motion carried by 52 votes to 32. Inquiries as to different plots of land and buildings were made, one of the lots being the Grouse Inn, owned by Mr. George Cheetham Hussey, but they were dropped, until on the 25th of April, 1883, a special general meeting of members empowered the committee to purchase a plot belonging to the executors of the late Robert Platt, at the corner of Huddersfield Road and Mottram Road. Mr. Gregory Gill was retained as architect, and Messrs. F. B. Wilde, James McCall, William Hall, and Samuel Bower Wood were elected a Building Committee. On the 9th November, 1883, the tender of Messrs. Garside, Barnes and Co. was accepted, and later Mr. A. Chorlton undertook to supply fixtures.

On the 20th June, 1884, Mr. J. H. Milligan was appointed branch manager, and when the time for commencing work there arrived the writer accompanied him as assistant, and Mr. Ernest Lees, the present manager of High Street Branch, became check boy. The first complete quarter, December, 1884, the sales at the new branch were £2,219, an average of £170 per week.

There had been inquiries made at different times from the beginning of 1880 until this year as to the

Former Members of Committee — William Hall, Thomas Beard, Geo. Britain, Thomas Knott, John Norris, W. H. Kenyon, Samuel Knight, John Allen, Squire Booth.

No. 4 Branch.—Huddersfield Road.

coal trade. In April, 1884, the neighbouring societies of Droylsden, Ashton, and Denton were visited by Mr. Wright Hadfield, and Mr. J. R. Jackson, secretary, for the purpose of obtaining information on the subject, and in August the same year one coal drop was rented. Two thousand tons of coal and two carts were bought in September, and by the 1st October the society was in a position to deliver loads of coal to members. The price of best round house coal was 7½d. per cwt., and double screened nuts 6½d. per cwt., delivered within certain limits; outside those limits ½d. per cwt. extra was charged, and members carrying coal by their own carts were supplied at ¼d. per cwt. less. Mr. Geo. Wilkinson, the present head of the coal department was, as a boy, appointed on the 29th September, 1884, to the coal office, and Mr. Edward Jones, the first carter, was appointed the same date. At the end of October a lorry was bought and the delivery of coal in bags commenced. Business increased and on the 26th December a second coal drop was rented. The average of the weekly sales, December quarter, was £38, in March it had risen to £59 per week.

CHAPTER XII.

1885 TO 1894—BOOTS SEPARATED FROM DRAPERY—MANCHESTER SHIP CANAL—SUBSCRIPTION TO CO-OPERATIVE UNION—BOOK CHECK SYSTEM ADOPTED—A STEP FORWARD IN MILLINERY AND DRESSMAKING—COAL WAGONS BOUGHT — STABLES ERECTED — EDUCATION FUND — NEWSROOM OPENED AND CLOSED—FIRE—BUTCHERING AGAIN—MR. F. E. MADEN, DRAPERY MANAGER—ELECTRIC LIGHT INSTALLED—3,000 MEMBERS—HEYROD BRANCH OPENED—MR. J. GREEN TAKES IN HAND TAILORING—DISTRESS IN COTTON TRADE ; WEEKLY GRANTS—FIRST SOIREE.

THE boot department was separated from drapery and opened in Back Grosvenor Street on the 30th March, 1885. Mr. J. H. Austerberry, the present manager of the department was appointed on the 13th March, and it was announced that boot repairing and clogging was undertaken. The sales in the department to June 10th were £670, an average of £67 per week. Since that time it has progressed until the turnover is nearly £5,000 a year. Amongst those who have contributed to this success in the boot department, in addition to Mr. Austerberry, may be mentioned Miss Crosby, who died in the society's service ; Miss

Boot Department.—Back Grosvenor Street.

Maden, who administered very efficiently the ladies' section for many years, commencing 1896 ; Miss Hannah Woolley, who was associated with her ; Mr. W. S. Stubbs, a practical bootmaker, who served the society well for some years and who is now boot department manager to Slaithwaite Society ; and Mr. J. B. Senior, also practical, the present energetic assistant.

The Manchester Ship Canal had the support of the members in 1884, a sum of £50 toward the Parliamentary expenses being voted on the 2nd April. On the 7th October, 1885, it was decided that 100 £10 shares be taken up, and in June, 1891, the last call was paid.

On the 1st October, 1884, the society's contribution to the funds of the Central Board of the Co-operative Union was increased from £5 to £10 per annum, the present contribution.

The metal checks were discarded in December, 1885, and the book system introduced. Deputations were appointed to visit Shaw, Oldham Equitable, and Mossley societies to see the book system in operation, and Harry Woolley and the writer were appointed to work it. From 1887 onward a proposal to dispense with the book system was several times put forward, but it survived until 1901, when the " Climax " system at present in use was commenced.

The sales in 1885 were £64,635, an increase of £4,691 over 1884 and £17,128 more than those of three years before. The dividend to members was £9,738, interest on shares £1,076, properties, &c., were written down £500, £46 was added to the reserve fund, and £40 was granted for educational purposes. Grants to the

Copley and other relief funds were made and there was a donation to the Co-operator Lifeboat No. 2.

At the end of 1885 a bolder step in the direction of millinery and dress and mantle-making was taken. A lady to undertake the management was advertised for, and on the 15th December Miss S. H. Seville was appointed. The department was opened Monday, 4th January, 1886, over drapery in Back Grosvenor Street, and from that date to the end of the first quarter, March 10th, the sales were £123. The first complete quarter ended June, the weekly average of sales in the department was £33. 19s. Miss Seville remained only a little over twelve months, and on the 15th March, 1887, a Stalybridge lady, Miss Swan, was appointed head dressmaker. Miss Swan resigned in August, 1890, and was succeeded by Mrs. Ingham. Less than two years later Mrs. Ingham left, and Mrs. Bradshaw was appointed in March, 1892. The department occasioned some anxiety, and more than once during the years 1886 to 1895 committees of inquiry were formed. On the last occasion they went so far as to close it. It was reopened in March, 1895, with Miss J. Lawton, of Mossley, in charge, and in their June report the committee wrote that it was very successful. Miss Lawton continued the management of dressmaking very efficiently until 1902.

It was in 1886 that coal wagons were first bought. The coal trade had been growing, the amounts paid for wagon hire were very large, and it was thought that a number of wagons would be a good investment. Twenty-three years' experience has amply proved that. Twelve wagons were ordered in April, 1886, this number was increased later, first to twenty and then to twenty-eight wagons, the present number. In December, 1889, the committee reported that twenty wagons had been running about $3\frac{1}{2}$ years and that they had cost to date, including repairs, £1,095. They had earned during the period £539, and had been written down in the accounts to £598. The policy of writing down the wagons out of their earnings has been followed to the present time, and after renewals and repairs have been met out of earnings there are still twenty-eight wagons in good running order and of good earning capacity valued in the books at less than 30s. each.

Another sign of growth at this time was the necessity for new stables. A tender by Messrs. Garside, Barnes and Company was accepted on the 7th May, 1886. The number of horses owned was increasing and it was thought advisable to hold one man responsible for them. In December the same year a clever horsekeeper in the person of Joseph Robinson was appointed. Mr. Robinson remained with the society until May, 1901, when he was succeeded by Mr. E. J. Yates. Mr. Yates was followed in March, 1903, by the present horsekeeper, Mr. David Warren, who is still so successful at the stables.

An education fund was raised in 1885 and 1886. Efforts in this direction had been made some years before. In April, 1877, the members in annual meeting decided that a reading-room be established, but it appears that the scheme was not proceeded with. Inquiry was made as to the number of reading-rooms in the town, and the question was again before the members' meeting in October, 1880. The meeting resolved, by 25 votes to 7, "That the proposal to establish a newsroom be not accepted," and it was decided at the same time that the sum of £50 set aside for education purposes be added to the reserve fund. Commencing in 1885 small grants of £3 to £20 from profits were made and a newsroom was opened on Monday, 4th January, 1886. It was not very successful. One reason, perhaps, was the fact that it was three flights up in the present Back Grosvenor Street building. Proposals to close it were brought forward at the quarterly meetings in April and July, 1886; they were negatived, but the agitation was kept up and in October, 1887, the opponents of the newsroom were successful and it was resolved that the reading-room be dispensed with. In June, 1888, the education fund was closed by the transfer of a small balance to the general reserve fund. This opposition to the newsroom could be better understood, perhaps, had the profits been precarious. At one of the same meetings, however, a sum of £192 from a single quarter's profits was set aside as a dividend reserve fund. In this year, 1886, a slight fire occurred. It originated in the office, some painters' material on a gas ring igniting. The borough fire brigade was called in, and by its aid the damage by fire was confined to the office. There was further damage by water, however, to the grocery and boot stocks beneath, and the claim on the Co-operative Insurance Society, which was promptly met, was £93.

In June, 1887, butchering appeared in the accounts for the first time since the 'sixties. A shop in High

CENTRAL BUTCHERING.—GROSVENOR STREET.

Street had been rented in March, and a competent butcher advertised for. Mr. Walter Ireland was appointed in April. A shop in Grosvenor Street owned by Mrs. Wilkinson was taken in October, and a cottage at Millbrook was converted to a butcher's shop in November. Mr. Ireland was succeeded by Mr. John Grayshan in January, 1888. The profits in butchering at this time were very small. In June, 1888, a dividend of 2¼d. only was made, and this had the effect of retarding the return to the coveted 3s. dividend. A general dividend of 2s. 9d. was declared. The following quarter, however, butchering made 11d., and the committee found themselves in a position to declare a dividend of 3s., with a balance of £45, which was added to the reserve fund. In April, 1889, the members accepted a recommendation of the committee that a butcher's shop be erected at Mount Pleasant, and the tender of Messrs. Garside, Barnes and Co. was accepted. Some two years later the house at Huddersfield Road Branch was altered, and became a butcher's shop. In 1893 this shop was closed and the premises were reconverted to a house. It appears there was no butchering at Huddersfield Road for four years, until in 1897 the present butchering branch was built in what was formerly a grocery unloading place. It was on the 22nd April, 1895, that Mr. Arthur Allen, the present butchering manager, was appointed, and since then, whatever difficulties the department has had to encounter it has always been felt that it is in safe hands.

At Heyrod butchering was carried on for many

years in the same shop as grocery, until in 1908 the present shop was built by Messrs. Wilson and Roberts. This completes the account of the establishment of butchering at the Central Stores and branches 1 to 5.

At the other branches, Kay Street, Cheetham Hill Road, and Stocks, butchering was provided for when the branches were built. The small shop at Millbrook was eventually given up, and in 1896 Messrs. Garside, Barnes and Co. built the existing shop in the grocery unloading place in Grenville Street. In 1897 the present Central butchering, No. 35, Grosvenor Street, and opposite Central grocery, was taken, and the shop first rented was given up. High Street butcher's shop was rebuilt by Mr. T. G. Shaw in 1898.

It has been mentioned that Mr. Frank E. Maden followed Miss Woolley as drapery manager. Mr. Maden had charge during a portion of the time that millinery and dressmaking was on its trial, and is remembered by many members, particularly ladies who came in contact with him in the shop, as a man of unfailing courtesy and one who gave admirable service. He left in September, 1889, to take the management of the drapery department of a larger society, and is at the time of writing with Eccles Society in that capacity. He was succeeded at Stalybridge by Mr. G. Fieldhouse, who remained with the society until 1894, and who proved a very keen buyer and manager.

Electric light was first adopted in 1890, Messrs. W. A. Shaw and Co., of Stockport, placing an installation in drapery and boots departments.

The membership reached 3,000 in September, 1891, and the sales for the year were £77,150.

No. 5 Branch.—Heyrod.

Heyrod Branch, No. 5, was opened in 1892, a shop and six cottages being purchased from Mrs. Garside in February. Mr. Fred Robinson, the present manager of Castle Hall Branch, took charge of the branch in April. The sales to June 11th were £259, and the first complete quarter £592.

It has been related how, in the 'sixties, tailoring agencies were taken up. About the beginning of 1886 arrangements were made with three Manchester houses for a tailor to attend in the drapery department two hours on each of two evenings per week and three hours on Saturdays. Members were supplied in this way with ready-made and bespoke garments, the representatives of the three firms taking measures, submitting samples and prices, and taking responsibility as to fit, &c. An important step forward was taken in 1891-2. A cutter was advertised for, and in February of the former year Mr. E. H. Field commenced his duties. Mr. Field did not remain long. On December 28th of the same year our present tailoring manager, Mr. Joseph Green, then of Haslingden, was appointed. A top floor at the rear of drapery was set apart, and there Mr. Green founded the tailoring and gentlemen's outfitting department as we know it to-day, a department which is eminently successful, and which, thanks to its manager and efficient staff, gives no anxiety.

In August, 1892, there was a tailors' lockout in the town, but the men working on the society's board were kept at work. The need of a ground floor shop was felt, and in November, 1894, No. 44, Melbourne Street, was taken. It was altered internally, and on

CO-OPERATION IN STALYBRIDGE.

March 29th the following year tailoring was removed there. This gave the department a fillip. The stock and staff were added to, and business increased until it was altogether too great for the premises. In June, 1900, the present commodious tailoring premises in Grosvenor Square were bought and refitted throughout. They were opened for business Friday, July 12th, 1901. Mr. Green had the training as cutters, amongst others, of Mr. T. A. Shaw, who filled for some time a position as cutter with Farnworth Society ; and of Mr. Walter Ellingworth, who is at present very successfully managing the tailoring department of the Prestwich Society. From that small beginning at the top of the Back Grosvenor Street building the department has grown until its turnover approaches £6,000 a year.

There was great distress amongst the workers in the cotton trade in 1892-3. In January of the latter year a scheme for weekly grants to distressed members was inaugurated. It was continued for eleven weeks, the society incurring an expenditure of £72, which was supplemented by a grant of £35 from the Co-operative Wholesale Society, making a total distribution of £107.

The last occasion on which the annual gathering of members took the form of a tea party and concert was in February, 1894. On the 23rd February, 1895, the first of the soirées was held in the Drill Hall. Mr. Wm. Wild provided an excellent concert, Mr. and Mrs. Nuttall contributed the humorous element, the old band played for dancing, and the veteran, Mr. John Duffy, acted as master of ceremonies. No fewer than 2,948 tickets were sold.

TAILORING.—GROSVENOR SQUARE

CHAPTER XIII.

1894 TO 1899—MR. J. H. HINCHLIFFE, SECRETARY—MR. J. B. MASON, MANAGER—MEMBERS VISIT THE " WHOLESALE "— OTHER EXCURSIONS — CONCERTS — ELECTRIC LIGHTING EXTENDED—CHEETHAM HILL ROAD PROPERTY—BUCKLEY STREET PROPERTY—LORD STREET PROPERTY—WAKEFIELD ROAD, HEYROD, PROPERTY — ADDITIONAL STABLES — BUILDING RULES — INFIRMARY COT — INDIAN FAMINE FUNDS—MILL OPERATIVES' DISTRESS FUND—ENGINEERS' LOCKOUT FUND—WEST OF IRELAND DISTRESS FUND— SMALL SAVINGS BANK—FIRST EXHIBITION—CASTLE HALL BRANCH OPENED—TELEPHONE—TECHNICAL SCHOOL GRANT —SOUTH AFRICAN WAR FUND—HELPING RESERVISTS' DEPENDENTS—VOLUNTEERS' PRIZE FUND—DEATH OF MR. JOHN HEAP.

IN February, 1894, the writer was appointed secretary in succession to Mr. J. R. Jackson, who had held the office since 1880. The new secretary's business career had been entirely with the society, first as check boy, then successively as grocery assistant, clerk, assistant secretary and treasurer, until, on the lamented death of his chief, the committee showed their confidence by appointing him to the vacancy.

Mr. J. B. Mason, the present general manager, was appointed on the 27th March, 1895, in succession to Mr. J. Mellor, who had been manager since 1876. Mr. Mason seemed from the first to have a conviction that everything depended on the turnover being kept up or increased. He set himself to augment it, and to his management is largely due the fact that the sales, which were £56,300 during a year immediately preceding his coming, have reached a total, imposing for a town of the size and with the population of Stalybridge, of £130,000, an increase of no less than 130 per cent in fifteen years. Whilst this increase has been making, the remuneration of the staff has not been overlooked. Substantial advances of wages have been made and the standard of efficiency has been raised.

There was a visit of members to the Balloon Street premises of the Co-operative Wholesale Society on Saturday, 30th March, 1895. The cost to each visitor, including railway fare and tea, was 1s. 6d. Six hundred persons went; they were conducted over the premises in small parties, and tea was served by the Wholesale Society.

On the 24th August of the same year there was an excursion to Alderley Edge, approximately 600 persons spending a very enjoyable day. Two trains were run, and the Ancient Shepherds' Reed Band accompanied the party. The trip was so popular that it was repeated on the 20th June, 1896. On this occasion the Stalybridge Old Band was engaged, and 454 adults and 55 children's fares were paid.

Another excursion in 1896 was to Hebden Bridge and Hardcastle Crags on the 22nd August. Tea was served by Hebden Bridge Society, and the accommodation was taxed to the utmost, the number of people who attended being nearly 1,000.

There were other excursions in the 'nineties, including one to Buxton in 1897, and another to Belle Vue in 1898. In connection with the latter, there was given a guarantee of 600 persons to tea.

From 1894 to 1899 the committee arranged concerts rather more freely. In addition to the annual gathering of members, there were concerts at the Oddfellows' Hall, Millbrook School, and other places. In September, 1895, and for several years, the theatre was hired for one evening, and there were some very large audiences. Popular prices were charged, varying from 1d. to 3d., with a small number of seats in the dress circle and stalls of the theatre at 1s. Mr. Charles Parker's Æolian Opera Company, of Rochdale, was booked for several of the large concerts. For the annual soirée, held March 5th, 1898, the Stalybridge Harmonic Society, with a band and chorus of 100 performers, was booked.

The electric lighting installation was extended at the end of 1895 by the Lancashire Electrical Engineering Company, of Ashton-under-Lyne. A new and larger dynamo, to light about 100 16-c.p. lamps, was put in; the premises were re-wired; and early the following year we had electric light in the office, boardroom, and grocery for the first time. The expenditure was a little over £200, and it was entirely written off the capital account from the profits of two quarters.

Cheetham Hill Road property, consisting of 23 houses and a shop, was bought in January, 1896;

seven houses in Buckley Street were purchased in October, 1897; Lord Street land was bought in July, 1897, and the erection of 15 houses thereon commenced early in 1898 by Mr. T. G. Shaw, with Mr. Geo. Rowbottom as architect; and in August, 1898, Mr. Tim Bradbury's tender for the erection of seven houses in Wakefield Road, Heyrod, was accepted, also under the superintendence of Mr. Rowbottom. In 1897 additional stables were built in the yard off Booth Street by Mr. A. Chorlton.

The building rules were adopted in 1897. Previously members could borrow money for building purposes under the general rules, but the special building rules provided for the advance by the society of a larger proportion of the purchase money, and in other ways have been conducive to a greater number of members becoming owners of the houses they occupy.

A subscription at the rate of 1d. per member per annum towards the maintenance of a children's cot in the Ashton District Infirmary was unanimously passed by the members in 1897. The cot is still maintained by Ashton, Stalybridge, and other neighbouring societies, and a good work is being done.

The same year there was a grant of £50 to an Indian Famine Fund. A similar grant was made three years later. The Co-operative Wholesale Society gave a donation of £1,000 to the 1897 fund, an action that our quarterly meeting approved.

Distress funds were somewhat numerous during the six years 1893 to 1898. The distribution of 1893 has been referred to. At quarterly meetings held January and April, 1896, there were appeals on behalf of the

CO-OPERATION IN STALYBRIDGE. 209

workpeople of Messrs. Adshead's and Messrs. Wilkinson's mills, and payments amounting to £69 were made. In November, 1897, a special meeting of members voted a sum of £100 as a donation to a local fund to aid people affected by an engineers' lockout, the payment to be spread over five weeks. The society was also asked to quote for a tea to be provided for the children of the engineers; 4d. per head was quoted, and the use of the hall granted for the 8th January, 1898. The Amalgamated Society of Engineers' Ashton, Stalybridge, Hyde and District Lockout Committee wrote tendering hearty thanks for the manner in which the children had been entertained, and for what they described as not the first generous action on the part of the society. Another appeal not made in vain was on behalf of a West of Ireland distress fund, raised locally, a contribution of £25 being made by a special meeting of members held 27th April, 1898.

The small savings bank was established in March, 1898. It has been an incentive to thrift on the part of the children of members. There is now £4,725 to the credit of depositors, a very large proportion of whom are children.

On Saturday, 22nd April, 1899, there was opened a three days' exhibition of articles produced by the Co-operative Wholesale and other productive societies, and the Castle Hall branch store was opened. His Worship the Mayor, Alderman Norman, performed the ceremony of opening the exhibition, and Mr. G. R. Patten, president of the society, discharged the function at the new premises.

At the exhibition there was a large attendance, the

assembly-room of the Town Hall being crowded. Mr. Patten presided, and was supported by the Mayor; Messrs. T. Knott, S. Knight, J. T. Bate, J. Allen, W. H. Kenyon, W. Wardle, E. P. Owens, and J. Heap, committee; J. H. Hinchliffe, secretary; J. B. Mason, manager; W. Thompson, treasurer; S. Hall and D. Holt, auditors; John Fawley, A. Hopwood, T. Beard; Geo. Rowbottom, architect of the new premises; Mr. F. Thompson, of Messrs. Buckley, Miller, and Thompson, solicitors to the society; Mr. W. Lander, of the Co-operative Wholesale Society; and delegates from neighbouring societies.

The Chairman said it gave him great pleasure to preside on that occasion, and to know that every article displayed in the hall had been produced under good conditions of labour, with a fair day's wages for a fair day's work. Co-operative production was cutting away one of the greatest curses of the country by its effect upon the sweating dens, where people were working early and late in insanitary workshops for a mere pittance. In doing that the co-operative system had rendered an important service to the public, and such an exhibition as they saw before them would in its results be of lasting importance. He would quote the words of Mr. Holyoake, who said: " Co-operation supplements political economy by organising the distribution of wealth. It touches no man's fortune, it seeks no plunder, it causes no disturbance in society; it gives no trouble to statesmen, it enters into no secret associations, it contemplates no violence, it subverts no order, it envies no dignity; it asks no favour, it keeps no terms with the idle, and it breaks no faith with the

No. 6 Branch.—Kay Street.

industrious; it means self-help, self-dependence, and such share of the common competence as labour shall earn, or thought can win, and these it intends to have." In the co-operative movement there were distributive and productive departments. The latter had not the advantage of the early start which the former had enjoyed, but to prove that there had been a great advance made he would give them some figures showing the progress recorded from 1883. In that year there were 15 societies, in 1893 there were 108, and in 1898 no fewer than 169. The sales of the 15 societies in 1883 amounted to £160,751, in 1893 the sales of the 108 were £1,292,668, and in 1897 the results of the 169 societies' operations came to £2,713,436. The capital of the societies in 1883 was £103,436, in 1893 £639,884, and in 1897 no less than £1,180,906. The figures he had given showed an increase of about fourteen fold in the same number of years.

He then introduced Alderman Norman, who had a cordial reception. He said he was pleased to see such a large gathering at the inauguration of the first exhibition of the Stalybridge Co-operative Society. It was a proof that the efforts of the committee were appreciated by the members. He had no doubt many members of the society and many of the public would attend to view the numerous articles so tastefully displayed. He looked upon it as his duty as Mayor of the borough to assist in any movement for the benefit of the people of the town. He had been very cosmopolitan. It had not mattered to him what class of politics or what sect, if the idea had been good and for the benefit of the inhabitants he had joined with it.

CO-OPERATION IN STALYBRIDGE.

The co-operative society of Stalybridge was strong and powerful, and the report before him showed that they were very successful. The sales during the past twelve months had been £84,765, and the carrying on of business with such a turnover meant industry and effort on the part of the committee for a nominal payment. Not only had the turnover been large, but so had the profit—£13,000 on £84,000. If such progress could be kept up he should expect, in the course of a few years, that the society would do a little more in aid of the charitable institutions of the town. The membership of the society was over 3,000, and represented some 15,000 persons, a large proportion of the inhabitants of the town. The co-operative movement nowadays touched almost every branch of trade, and he understood the opening of the Castle Hall Branch would make the sixth connected with the Stalybridge Society. Amongst the departments of the society he noticed they had one which dealt with the building or buying of houses by the members. The Government was bringing in a Bill by which municipal authorities would be able to advance money to any person on suitable security for the purchase or erection of his own dwelling. It might tell somewhat against co-operative societies, but personally he did not care which way it went, so long as he could see people living in their own houses, because he believed that the more people lived in their own houses the better they would know their responsibilities, and the better it would be for the sanitary and moral arrangements of the town. (Hear, hear.) He had great pleasure in declaring the exhibition open. (Applause.)

Mr. J. T. Bate proposed a vote of thanks to Alderman Norman. During the past 15 months, he said, the building contracts let by the society amounted to about £10,000, all to Stalybridge contractors. The society employed 86 persons, and paid wages which averaged £1. 1s. per week all round, a sum which he thought was very good when they considered the number of young persons employed.

Mr. W. Wardle seconded, and Mr. W. Lander supported the motion, both gentlemen speaking of the benefits conferred by the co-operative societies of the country. On the proposition of Mr. J. Fawley, seconded by Mr. Hopwood, thanks were given to Mr. Patten for his services in the chair. During the three days the exhibition was open there was an excellent programme of music by an orchestral band, conducted by Mr. T. Cheetham, with Mr. J. Hulme as leader.

The *Stalybridge Reporter* of April 29th, 1899, had the following comments :—

> The Stalybridge Co-operative Society is to be complimented upon the success which attended the exhibition of co-operative productions, and upon the magnificent stores erected in Kay Street. During the time the exhibition was open some thousands of people visited it. After the opening of the exhibition on Saturday, the officials of the society, together with a number of members, proceeded to Kay Street for the opening of the Castle Hall branch store. Mr. John Heap called upon Mr. Geo. Rowbottom, the architect, who presented a gold key to Mr. G. R. Patten, president. Mr. Patten complimented Mr. Rowbottom and the contractors (Messrs. Shuttleworth Brothers) for the admirable manner in which they had carried out the work. He returned thanks for the gift, and observed that they had erected those new premises on account of the steady progress the society had made during the past four

years. The inscription on the key was as follows:—
"Presented to George Patten, Esq., of Heyrod, at the opening of the Castle Hall Branch of the Stalybridge Industrial Co-operative Society Ltd., George Rowbottom, Esq., architect, April, 1899." The premises were then inspected, and afterwards tea was served in the society's hall.

The following description was given:—

The new building consists of a fine grocer's shop, with a flour store behind, a butcher's shop, and two dwelling houses. The grocer's shop is entered at the angle of Brierley Street and Kay Street, and is fitted up with all the latest improvements. The whole of the interior of the butcher's shop is faced with opalite treated in various shades of colour, and presents a beautiful appearance. The building is arranged to suit the special needs of the site. The design is treated in a free, classical manner, the walls being faced with Accrington bricks, with dressings of polished Yorkshire stone. The work was carried out by Messrs. Shuttleworth Brothers, the sub-contractors being Messrs. Myles and Warner (brickwork), Mr. T. G. Shaw (joiners' work), Messrs. Pickles Brothers (slating), Messrs. W. H. Whitehead and Sons (plumbing and painting), and Messrs. Mellor and Walker (plastering).

The same year (1899) the telephone was installed, the society becoming a subscriber to the National Telephone Company, and having all the branches and Central put in communication with each other by means of private lines.

Efforts in the direction of an education department had not achieved so much as those of some other societies. Newsrooms had been opened, and after a brief spell closed, and little or nothing had been attempted in the formation of classes such as are carried on successfully by many societies. In 1899 a small grant for educational purposes was used in another manner, a sum of £25 being handed over to the Stalybridge Technical Instruction Committee. To form a connecting link between elementary and continuation classes there had been offered free admission to the technical school to a certain number of children attending day and evening classes, limited to grant-earning classes. The society's grant was used to extend to commercial classes what was already done for the others, the subjects specially named for encouragement being cotton-spinning, shorthand, book-keeping, typewriting, dressmaking, millinery, and cookery. The grant has been repeated yearly. The principal of the school reported in 1906 that by means of the grant 104 free scholarships had been awarded to students who had acquitted themselves well in the various examinations, and, in addition to that, 93 scholarships had been granted to pupils who were entering the school for the first time. Any pupil, he said, of any promise, who worked and had the necessary ability, could by means of the grant obtain free admission and pass through the various stages of the subject free of cost. The scholarships were thoroughly appreciated by the students, and had an excellent effect on their attention and application to their studies.

A fund to aid the dependents of army reservists who had gone to the front in the South African War was raised in the town in 1899. In November the members voted a sum of £50. In addition to this there was granted to the wife, children, or dependents of each member who had been called up for active service goods to the value of 10s. per week, except where they were otherwise provided for. Members of the committee met to receive applications. From November, 1899, to September quarter, 1902, when the last of the reservists returned from the front, the dependents of nine men received £376, and there was evidence from the men themselves that great good had been done by the timely help. Mr. W. Wardle was a member of the War Fund Committee for the town.

In January, 1901, the members passed a contribution of £5 to the volunteers—now territorial force—prize fund, a contribution which has been repeated yearly to date.

In their report of June, 1900, the committee expressed their deep regret at the death, which occurred on the 2nd May, of Mr. John Heap. Mr. Heap had been officially connected with the society for the long period of 27 years, and was a member of the Board until his death.

CHAPTER XIV.

1900 TO 1907--CHEETHAM HILL ROAD BRANCH—"CLIMAX" CHECK SYSTEM—WORK FOR TRADE-UNIONISTS ONLY — SPECTACLES, &C., AGENCY—MANCHESTER ROYAL INFIRMARY—CHILDREN'S HOSPITAL—SOCIETY FOR PREVENTION OF CRUELTY TO CHILDREN—CHILDREN'S GALA—MILLINERY IN MELBOURNE STREET—SIX FIGURES OF SALES—INCREASED PRODUCTION—DEATH OF MR. S. KNIGHT— ABATTOIR — MOUNT PLEASANT BRANCH EXTENDED — DEFENCE FUND — BOROUGH EDUCATION COMMITTEE — EXCURSION TO LONDON—DEATH OF MR. WM. HALL— COTTON SHORTAGE AND DECREASE IN TURNOVER—COTTON GROWING ASSOCIATION—CONVALESCENT HOMES—ANOTHER LOCAL DISTRESS FUND — DELEGATES' APPOINTMENT — OFFICE OF TREASURER ABOLISHED—SUNDRIES SOCIETY DIRECTORATE — PRINTING SOCIETY SHARES — STRATFORD EXCURSION—CORN MILLS TAKEN OVER BY THE WHOLESALE SOCIETY—PREMIER MILLS—ELECTRIC MOTORS—KNITTING MACHINERY—MR. J. T. BATE RESIGNS—PRESIDENT A MAGISTRATE — BOOK-KEEPING CLASS — MISS FIRTH, MILLINER — MISS HOLT, DRESSMAKER — INTEREST ON SHARES.

CHEETHAM Hill Road Branch, No. 7, was opened 1900. Fully eight years before there had been a proposal to open a branch store in or near Lodge Lane, Dukinfield, the committee agreeing to recommend such a scheme. It did not go forward, however, until

October, 1898, when the members decided that it should be opened in Cheetham Hill Road. In May, 1899, the tender of Messrs. Saxon Brothers was accepted, and soon work was commenced, with Mr. Geo. Rowbottom as architect. The branch was opened February 19th, 1900, with Mr. W. Broadbent as branch manager. During the three weeks to the end of March quarter the sales were £213, and the first complete quarter (June, 1900) they were £1,013.

In January, 1901, a deputation, which included the writer, visited Farnworth, where the " Climax " check system, as at present in operation at Stalybridge, was originated. A report to a special meeting of members was given on February 6th ; the system was adopted, and on the 11th March was introduced in the shops. In September the same year Mr. Albert Shaw was appointed to take charge of the check office. He was a man who knew exactly what was required to ensure the successful operation of the system, and he is still conducting very efficiently that important department of the office.

A resolution of the committee of the 14th June, 1901, will be appreciated by all trade-unionists. It was to the effect that no work would in future be given to any tradesman who did not comply with the rules and regulations of his trade society.

In June quarter, 1901, the society commenced to act as agent to Messrs. Cowan and Sons, the eminent optologists, of Manchester. Since that date many members have had the advantage of the best possible advice from Messrs. Cowan in the selection of spectacles, eyeglasses, artificial eyes, &c.

No. 7 Branch.—Cheetham Hill Road, Dukinfield.

The same year, at the October quarterly meeting, the present annual subscription of £10 to the Manchester Royal Infirmary was passed.

A year later the annual subscription of £2 to the Manchester Children's Hospital at Pendlebury was fixed.

A donation of £5 to the National Society for the Prevention of Cruelty to Children had been made yearly for some eight years, and another, similar in amount, to the Stalybridge Sick Nursing Society since 1899.

The children's gala was inaugurated in 1901, the first being held August 24th.

The removal of tailoring to a front position in Melbourne Street six years before had been so advantageous to that department that it was thought when tailoring was removed to the larger premises in Grosvenor Square the shop vacated could be utilised to good purpose for millinery. Miss Bruce was engaged in August, 1901, and on the 3rd October millinery was taken into Melbourne Street under her management. A very smart millinery business was done there. There were disadvantages, however, in drapery and millinery being so far apart, and some four years later the drapery premises were partly reconstructed internally, and millinery was again removed to its present position in Back Grosvenor Street.

Six figures of sales were reached for the first time in 1901, the total being £105,242, £6,947 over that of 1900 and the highest then attained. The dividend to members was £15,591, and interest on their shares £2,024. One hundred and three persons were em-

224 CO-OPERATION IN STALYBRIDGE.

ployed. Seven years before the wages paid to productive workers in millinery, dressmaking, tailoring, and bootmaking totalled £600 ; in 1901 the amount was £1,539, an increase of 156 per cent.

The committee referred with sorrow in their report of September, 1902, to the death of Mr. Samuel Knight, which occurred on the 16th September. For thirteen years at least they had known Mr. Knight as an earnest co-operator and a conscientious man, his connection with the Board dating back to 1889.

In this year a small building off Robinson Street, rented for the purposes of an abattoir, was given up, and the existing commodious premises at the rear of Buckley Street property were built by Messrs. W. Storrs, Sons and Co.

Mount Pleasant Branch was extended backward by Messrs. Shuttleworth Brothers.

A defence fund, for the purpose of counteracting the despicable boycotting tactics of certain traders in St. Helens and other towns was raised at this time by the Co-operative Union. A special meeting of members held Wednesday, October 8th, 1902, unanimously voted a sum of £100. It was suggested that for the movement there was nothing to fear, the boycott having the effect eventually of increasing the membership and turnover of the societies attacked ; but that there should be a contribution to the fund for the sake of individual co-operators who had been dismissed from their employment and in other ways victimised. The directors of the Co-operative Wholesale Society had proposed to guarantee a sum of £50,000. The proposal was approved by the societies, and the fund

CO-OPERATION IN STALYBRIDGE. 225

of £100,000 desired by the Union was very soon guaranteed. There is still a defence committee of the Union prepared to take action if required. Four calls upon the societies have been made, in proportion to the amounts guaranteed, amounting together to 6 per cent of the fund. Thus Stalybridge Society has been called upon for £6 only, and there is still available, nearly seven years after the raising of the fund, a sum of £94,000.

In March, 1903, Mr. J. B. Mason, general manager to the society, was nominated as the society's representative on the Education Committee of the borough, a position he still holds.

An excursion to London, joint with Ashton Society, was run this year, leaving Stalybridge on Whit-Friday night and returning Whit-Saturday night. The inclusive charge for fare, breakfast, tea, and some six hours' driving was 17s. 6d. each person. Breakfast was served by the Co-operative Wholesale Society's London Branch, and the arrangements for rail journey, tea, and drive were made by Messrs. Dean and Dawson. Stalybridge sent 119 passengers; including those from Ashton, there were 300.

In August, 1903, the committee had to regret the loss by death of another colleague, Mr. William Hall, who died on the 3rd. He was a man, they said, of long experience in the movement, having been elected to the Board so long before as 1876.

The shortage of American cotton was responsible for a decrease in the turnover, the first for nine years, in 1903. The total sales were £107,671, compared with £109,930 in 1902. A hope was expressed that the great work of the British Cotton Growing Association would meet with success. A contribution of £50 to the funds of the association was passed by the members at their January, 1904, meeting.

The North-Western Co-operative Convalescent Homes Association was registered about this time, and in January, 1904, the members decided to apply for 85 £1 shares. The shares are not withdrawable, and do not bear interest. There are two homes, one at Blackpool and one at Otley in Yorkshire. A good number of Stalybridge members have had residence at the homes as convalescents and visitors, and all who have reported have testified to the excellence of the arrangements. Another convalescent home which many members have utilised to advantage is owned by the Co-operative Wholesale Society and situated at Roden, near Shrewsbury.

At the beginning of 1904 another fund for the relief of distress in the borough was raised, on this occasion by the Mayor. The committee made a grant of £10. On April 6th the members confirmed the action and voted a further sum of £40, to be paid as the committee thought fit. It appears that the society was not called upon for the full amount, the fund being closed when £30 had been paid.

The annual meeting, April, 1904, resolved that delegates to meetings of societies or companies of which the society was a shareholder be appointed partly by the committee and partly by the members at annual meetings, and that they report to quarterly meetings. The delegates under this arrangement are now Messrs. James Harrison, Geo. Heathcote, A.

Longden (one of the joint jubilee secretaries), and F. J. Nash.

Until 1905 there had been elected as treasurer, with the exception of about one year, 1893 to 1894, one not on the permanent staff. Mr. John Ridgway has been referred to as the holder of the office. He was followed by Mr. J. B. W. Buckley in 1885, then came Mr. Wm. Backhurst in 1888, and the writer, who was on the staff, from 1893 to 1894, and who relinquished the office on his appointment to the secretaryship. Mr. Wm. Thompson followed in 1894. The duties were very conscientiously performed by Mr. Thompson for some eleven years, until April, 1905, when he retired, and it was arranged that the work should in future be undertaken by one of the office staff. Mr. A. E. Jackson, then chief clerk, was the first to take office under the new arrangement, and he held it until he left the society's service in 1907, when he was appointed secretary to Fleetwood Society. He was succeeded by Mr. Edwin Wright, the present cashier.

The Co-operative Sundries Manufacturing Society Limited, of Droylsden, elected Mr. John Fawley, our present chairman, at a meeting of shareholders held March, 1905, to the seat he still holds on the board of directors.

The same quarter 100 £1 shares of the Co-operative Printing Society Limited were taken up.

On Whit-Saturday, June 17th, 1905, Ashton, Stalybridge, and Hyde societies ran another joint excursion, conducted by Messrs. Dean and Dawson. On this occasion it was to Stratford-on-Avon, the birthplace of Shakespeare, and the arrangements included a drive to Warwick and Leamington, with breakfast at Stratford, and tea after the drive. The inclusive charge for fare, drive, breakfast, and tea was 11s. 3d. There were 78 passengers from Stalybridge, 43 from Hyde, and 150 from Ashton.

The Star (Oldham) and Rochdale corn mills were taken over by the Co-operative Wholesale Society in 1906. There was a small loss on realisation of the Rochdale shares, but the Star Mill had been so prosperous that there was a substantial profit on the whole. The amount at credit of our share account in the books of the Rochdale Corn Mill Society was £412, and the shares realised £364; the Star Corn Millers' Society had £503 to our credit as shares, which brought in £909. Thus there was a net profit on the two lots of shares of £358, which was added to the reserve fund.

In April, 1906, the members discussed a proposal to take up shares of the Premier Mills Limited. Three years before there had been a suggestion that shares of the Victor Mill Limited should be applied for, but it was negatived. Of the Premier, 1,000 £5 shares were taken up, and the society nominated Mr. Thomas Knott for the board of directors of the company. He remained on the directorate until his death in October, 1908, when he was succeeded by Mr. R. Firth, who is still in office.

Electric motors for hoisting, coffee-grinding, &c., and electric irons for dressmakers' use, were introduced in 1906. The latter were not a great success, and their use was discontinued in 1909, but the motors are still in use. Current is taken, not from the society's dynamo, but from the Tramways Board.

Another development in a small way in 1906 was the introduction of a Harrison knitting machine in drapery.

At the annual meeting in April, 1906, Mr. J. T. Bate resigned his seat on the Board in consequence of his appointment as manager of the Roy Mill, Royton. The committee expressed their regret at the loss of his services, and said their hearty good wishes would go with him.

In November the same year Mr. William Wardle, the society's president, was appointed to the magisterial bench of the borough.

A book-keeping class, open to the staffs of all departments, was commenced in earnest in October, 1906, the committee granting the use of the hall. Mr. A. E. Jackson was teacher, and he had students of both sexes. At the end of the term an examination paper was set by the writer, and several students acquitted themselves well. They showed their appreciation of Mr. Jackson's services by a presentation.

Millinery passed into the hands of its present head in 1906. Miss Bruce was followed by Miss Hollinshead, and on the retirement of the latter in 1906, Miss Firth, who still controls the department successfully, was appointed to take charge of the workroom, with Miss R. Roberts responsible for the showroom and sales.

Dressmaking, too, passed under new management the same year. Miss Lawton was succeeded by Miss Leach in 1902; then followed Miss Schofield, March, 1904; Miss Wood, March, 1906; and finally the indefatigable Miss S. Holt, who is still in charge.

The present rule as to interest on share capital was passed by the members January 2nd, 1907. The matter had been many times discussed. As far back as April, 1885, Mr. James Bamforth moved that the rate of interest be reduced from 5 to 4 per cent. In July, 1886, the minimum quarter's trade of a member to secure the full rate of interest, still 5 per cent, was fixed at £2, the rate to be 2½ per cent to members not complying with the rule as to trade. In October, 1893, there was a motion to the effect that a member trading to the extent of £2 a quarter be paid 5 per cent on £10, £3 trade 5 per cent on £15, and so on; and in October, 1894, there was an effort to raise the minimum trade to £4. The committee had before the members in April, 1905, a recommendation that the rate of interest on all shares be reduced to 4⅙ per cent, and that a member's quarter's trade to entitle him to that rate be raised to £4. The members accepted that part of the resolution which referred to the raising of the minimum trade, but the rate of interest payable to those who did the necessary trade remained through all those years at what it is in 1909, 5 per cent. It was thought by many members that the provision for £4 minimum trade was a hardship, and in January, 1907, a special meeting of members accepted Mr. John Fernley's proposal to the effect that £2 trade a quarter should entitle a member to 5 per cent up to £20 shares, £3 trade 5 per cent up to £30, £4 trade 5 per cent up to £40.

CHAPTER XV.

1907 TO 1909—UNION NEW HEADQUARTERS—WHAT THE UNION HAS DONE—SUNDRIES SOCIETY'S NEW WORKS— A BANKING ACCOUNT WITH THE WHOLESALE SOCIETY— ADDING BY MACHINERY—" OUR CIRCLE "—DEATH OF MR. JAMES BAILEY—SALES 1907, £129,537—COMMITTEE ELECTIONS — CANVASSING — CO-OPERATIVE INSURANCE SOCIETY—ASHTON DISTRICT INFIRMARY—DEATH OF MR. THOMAS KNOTT—CASTLE HALL MILL BOUGHT—STORY OF DRAPERY CONTINUED—MR. T. FAULKNER, DRAPERY MANAGER—STOCKS BRANCH, NO. 8—SUNDRIES SOCIETY REFERRED TO — £100 SHARES ALLOTTED — COLLECTIVE ASSURANCE—JUBILEE COMMITTEE.

THE Co-operative Union had under consideration a scheme for new headquarters, and there was an appeal to the societies for a sum of £20,000 to secure a site and erect a building to be styled "Holyoake House," near those of the Co-operative Wholesale Society in Manchester. It was suggested that societies should contribute at the rate of 3d. per member. Stalybridge Society's contribution at that rate was £46, and at the annual meeting held 3rd April, 1907, the members readily passed it. A brief account of what the Union is and what it has done may be useful here. The Co-operative Union is an institution charged with the duty of keeping alive and diffusing a knowledge of the principles which form the life of the co-operative movement, and giving to its active members, by advice and instruction—literary, legal, or commercial—the help they may require. Most of the legal advantages enjoyed by co-operators have been attained by the Union. Amongst those advantages are (1) the right of the societies of holding in their own names lands and buildings, and property generally, and of suing and being sued in their own names instead of being driven to the employment of trustees; (2) the power to hold £200 instead of £100 by individual members; (3) the limitation of the liability of members; (4) the exemption of societies from charge to income tax on profits under the condition that the number of their shares shall not be limited; (5) the extension of the power of members to bequeath shares, loans, and deposits up to £100 by nomination, without the formality of a will or the necessity of appointing executors.

The Co-operative Sundries Society commenced the erection of new works at Droylsden about this time, and on the 2nd October, 1907, our members accepted a recommendation of the committee that 200 additional £1 shares of the Sundries Society be taken up, and that a further sum of £200 be placed as a loan. The new building was opened February 13th, 1909, and we were represented at the opening ceremony.

As early as 1880, and again in 1889, it had been suggested that a banking account with the Co-opera-

CO-OPERATION IN STALYBRIDGE.   235

tive Wholesale Society should be opened. The suggestion was not then adopted. On the 17th June, 1907, however, it was arranged that such an account should be opened, and from a date shortly after that all the society's banking business has been done through the Wholesale Society.

A Burroughs adding machine was bought in June, 1907, and since that date members' purchases have been added by machinery. It is used for many other purposes; it saves an immense amount of time and brain-fag; it never makes a mistake; and it seems now quite indispensable.

The same year the first issue of the admirable children's journal, "Our Circle" appeared. A good order was given, and copies were placed for sale in all the shops.

Mr. James Bailey, of Millbrook, died in 1907. He had been on the Board so recently as July, 1906. A letter of condolence was sent to the family.

The year 1907 was the best the society had experienced. The sales were £129,537, an increase of £10,982 on 1906, the previous highest. The dividend to members was £19,232, and the interest on their shares £2,454.

The subject of committee elections was brought forward at members' meetings time after time. In April, 1884, there was a resolution to the effect that the committee retire one quarterly, not three annually as hitherto. Two years later Mr. Wm. Brown moved—
" That retiring members be not eligible for re-election until they have been off the Board four quarters." The motion was negatived. In April, 1886, Mr. T. Ken-

worthy proposed—"That the members of Millbrook should have the power to nominate one or more members to represent their district." This carried, and Mr. Thomas Wood, of Millbrook, was elected at the same meeting. In January, 1893, Mr. M. Naden was successful with a motion in favour of standing down, and in July, 1895, there was an unsuccessful effort to reverse that decision. A motion in October, 1897— "That Millbrook and Heyrod members each have a representative, that in each case he be elected by his branch only, and that the members of those two branches do not vote in any other election" was rejected by 82 votes to 27. In October, 1898, and January, 1904, there were efforts to revert to the system of yearly elections, but they were defeated, and quarterly elections took place until 1908, when Mr. Allen Hopwood's proposal of the present rule was accepted. This provides for the election and retirement of three members half-yearly, each to serve eighteen months, to be eligible for re-election for a second term of eighteen months, and after that to stand down for twelve months; Millbrook and Heyrod branches to have jointly one representative.

There were efforts, too, to put a stop to canvassing, by making it a disqualification, in April, 1900, January, 1907, and January, 1909. On the last of the three dates Mr. A. Hopwood's motion on the subject was passed unanimously.

The Co-operative Insurance Society Limited had new offices in Corporation Street, Manchester, erected about this time, and in April, 1908, Mr. J. Fawley and Mr. A. E. Dickin represented us at the opening.

At a very early stage the committee had given their support to the Co-operative Insurance Company as it was formerly styled. There was a resolution December 31st, 1866—" That the society join the conference to consider the mutual insurance proposition." Probably the conference here referred to would be one of the early steps toward the formation of the Insurance Society, which was registered in 1867. In November, 1867, it was decided that the society become a member of the company; there was a first call of 1s. per share in April, 1868, and further calls amounting to 4s. per share, the present amount per share called-up. Our holding was increased, first to 50, and in 1881 to 65 shares, at which it still stands. In February, 1869, the society's buildings and stock were insured with the company for £1,500. From that the business we have given to the Insurance Society has increased until the amount insured is many thousands of pounds in fire, fidelity, and other departments, including the insurance against fire of all the branch stores and a good proportion of the Central premises risk, the latter being partly reinsured in other fire offices. A member of the society, Mr. Samuel Hibbert, was acting as agent to the insurance company in 1889. Afterwards there was a long interval during which there was no agent for Stalybridge. In 1908 Mr. James Harrison, of Millbrook, was appointed an agent.

The Ashton District Infirmary has had the society's support since 1870, a donation of £5 being passed by the annual meeting of May 2nd. Later an annual subscription of five guineas was paid; it was increased in April, 1886, to ten guineas; in July, 1908, it was again doubled, the present subscription of twenty guineas per annum being fixed.

On the 2nd October, 1908, the committee passed a vote of condolence with the family of the late Thomas Knott, who had died suddenly the day before. A similar vote was passed by the quarterly meeting of members, October 7th.

The old Castle Hall Mill was offered for sale to the society in August, 1902. The offer was not accepted. In 1908 it was again offered; on the 4th May the conveyance was sealed and the mill became the property of the society. At the time of writing there is no definite scheme, but it is thought that the site may at some future time be used for an extension to the Central premises.

The story of the drapery department to 1894 has been told. In that year Mr. J. T. Evans became drapery manager; he remained until 1905. Mr. Evans was succeeded by Mr. A. V. Cartlidge, who came to us from a Yorkshire society in 1902. Mr. Cartlidge was very energetic and the department flourished under his care. He was drapery manager from June, 1905, to June, 1908. The sales for a year immediately preceding his taking charge were £8,378; during the last year of his management they were £12,518. He left with good credentials to take the management of drapery for Peterborough Society. Mr. T. Faulkner, who was appointed first counterman when Mr. Cartlidge took the management, and who became drapery manager on the resignation of the latter, has proved a worthy successor.

Drapery, Dressmaking, and Millinery.—Back Grosvenor Street.

CO-OPERATION IN STALYBRIDGE. 241

The annual meeting of members held 1st April, 1908, adopted the recommendation of the committee that a branch store, No. 8, for grocery and butchering, be erected in Taylor Street, Stocks Lane, Stalybridge. A plot of land fronting Taylor Street and French Street on the Stamford Estate was taken. Messrs. Saxon Brothers and Co. Limited undertook the builders' work and Mr. Arthur Mee the plumbers', with Mr. Geo. Rowbottom as architect. The branch was opened on Saturday, December 5th, 1908, under the management of Mr. Garnet Guthrie. There were present at the opening Mr. John Fawley, president; Messrs. R. Hanson, W. Shaw, T. W. Barnett, Hugh Lawton, A. Cooper, R. Stubbs, E. P. Owens, and A. E. Dickin, committee; Mr. J. H. Hinchliffe, secretary; Mr. J. B. Mason, manager; Mr. D. Holt, auditor; Mr. A. Turner, of the committee of Ashton-under-Lyne Society; Mr. Geo. Backhurst, manager of the Co-operative Sundries Society; Messrs. J. Saxon and O. Andrew, of Saxon Bros. and Co. Limited, builders of the branch; Mr. A. Mee, plumbing contractor; Mr. Geo. Rowbottom, architect; and others. Mr. Barnett called upon Mr. Rowbottom, who said the new store had been constructed in such a manner as to ensure cleanliness and to avoid interference with business whilst any necessary decoration was going on. He trusted it would do all the society expected, and more, and that further extension would soon be necessary. (Hear, hear.) He had very great pleasure in presenting to Mr. Fawley the key. Mr. Fawley thanked Mr. Barnett for his introduction, and Mr. Rowbottom for his handsome present—the key. It was at the request, he said, of a large number of members in that district that the committee decided to build that branch. It was in a populous district and a growing one, and he believed it would prove one of the best of the branches. Speaking as he was to co-operators he need no more than mention one or two of the advantages to be derived by members of a society. They participated quarterly in proportion to their purchases, in the dividend, which would otherwise be profit going to one or a few. They knew how useful that dividend was. For one who was bringing up a young family it would probably clothe the children, or provide a trip to the seaside; or if it were left in as share capital at interest it would be there for any emergency such as sickness or bad trade, or disputes such as had just been experienced in the cotton trade. He had no doubt many members had felt recently the advantage of having such capital. He was connected with a productive concern at Droylsden, the Co-operative Sundries Society. The workers there were employed under the most favourable conditions, and they participated half-yearly in a bonus to labour. Everyone who worked for the Sundries Society received 1s. 6d. in the £ bonus on his wages. No young man of 21 or over, whatever his occupation, had less than 24s. a week, and with bonus that was increased to 25s. 9d. a week. His hearers would find in their new shop that afternoon a fair show of the goods made at Droylsden and at the productive works of their great Co-operative Wholesale Society. The Stalybridge Society had been very successful in other parts ; he believed Stocks Lane people would prove that they were good co-operators

STOCKS BRANCH, No. 8.

and would make that enterprise a huge success. He had pleasure in opening No. 8 Branch of the Stalybridge Co-operative Society. Mr. Fawley then unlocked the door and the shop was at once crowded by purchasing members.

Additional withdrawable shares were allotted, commencing April, 1909, making the maximum holding per member £100. It appears that in 1881 the society went to the limit imposed by Act of Parliament, as much as £200 shares being allotted to individual members. In April of that year there was a proposal to reduce it to £100, and in the following year notice was given that shares over £100 held by any one member would cease to bear interest from the 1st April, 1882. There was a resolution, January, 1885, further reducing it to £50, but this was rescinded a year later. The limit became £90 in April, 1886, and later it was lowered by £10 at a time, until in February, 1890, it was £40. That limit was retained until the April, 1909, meeting carried unanimously Mr. A. E. Dickin's motion that it be raised to £100, the maximum under the rules then in force, the rate of interest to remain at 5 per cent up to £40, and to be 3 per cent on the remaining £60.

The Co-operative Insurance Society's Collective Life Assurance scheme was referred to at the same meeting. Nearly five years before we entertained the conference of the Oldham District, North-Western Section of the Co-operative Union, and "Collective Assurance" was the subject, Mr. James Odgers, secretary to the Insurance Society, reading a paper. The scheme was not then taken up in Stalybridge. In other places it made headway until in April, 1909, 118 societies had it in operation. Then the members accepted Mr. James Hibbert's motion requesting the committee to obtain further information as to the scheme, with a view to its being adopted. Under the scheme, if it is adopted, the lives of all members will be assured by one policy, the premium of 1d. per £1 of sales being paid by the society. The experience so far is that the premium is reduced eventually by surpluses to about ¾d. per £1. The expenses charged to the collective department by the Insurance Society are limited to 5 per cent of the premiums. What a great saving is effected will be apparent when it is realised how great is the expense of industrial life assurance where the premium is collected in weekly instalments from house to house. The average benefit secured for a premium of £1 so collected is 11s. 5d. only; by means of the collective method of the Co-operative Insurance Society members may secure 19s. benefit for every £1 of premium paid.

For the purpose of carrying out the jubilee celebration the annual meeting of April, 1908, appointed a committee consisting of the General Committee, the manager, secretary, and six other members—Messrs. John Woolley, Joe Ollerenshaw, George Barrett, A. Longden, George Heathcote, and Arthur Hamer. Three months later it was decided that the jubilee fund, already accumulating, should be increased to £1,000. Mr. W. Wardle, J.P., and Mr. A. Longden became jubilee secretaries, and the committee set to work.

PART III.

The Jubilee Celebration.

AGED MEMBERS' PARTY.

DURING the jubilee year smoking concerts were held. The first function in the scheme of the jubilee committee, however, was a gathering of aged members—from sixty years of age upwards—on Saturday, 27th February, 1909. Including members and husbands and wives of members, some 450 tickets were applied for, and just about 400 persons attended, although the weather was somewhat severe. Tea was served in Old St. George's School, and at the Town Hall they were entertained by Mrs. A. N. Turner (soprano), Mr. T. Shaw (bass), Mr. Sam Hill (the local elocutionist), Mr. Sam Fitton and Mr. George Hilton (humorists), and Mr. J. Cropper (pianist).

At the Town Hall Mr. John Fawley was chairman. In a pithy address, he said it was the society's jubilee year, and it had been decided that certain festivities should take place to celebrate that jubilee. It was considered that the older members were the first entitled to recognition, because they in years gone by had done a good deal to strengthen and sustain the society, and to bring it up to what it was that day. In May there would be held an exhibition of articles made in co-operative manufactories, just to show the members and the public what was produced by co-operators, with co-operators' capital, for co-operators. Other parties would be held, but the one which to his mind was most important, and to which he looked with the greatest hope of success, was the one which would be held in June—the demonstration, procession, and field day for the children of members. He trusted everybody would help during those months ; would do all they could to strengthen the hands of the committee ; and so contribute towards a general success that jubilee year. Fifty years ago the society had started, with a decision to supply the wants of the working people. It was seen even in those early days that there were many opportunities and advantages for working people in co-operation. It was a banding together of working men that started the movement in Stalybridge. They were men of ability, of courage, and of determination. In the early stages they had to prove to the people that co-operation was beneficial and necessary to the workers. The society had in the early years many difficulties, many trials. The American war broke out, and many there that night would remember the great trials and privations of those in the cotton manufacturing towns of Lancashire in consequence of the war between North and South. The society at that time was struggling very hard indeed, but the men in charge were not easily daunted

CO-OPERATION IN STALYBRIDGE. 251

by obstacles. The society had grown until it was the most powerful and influential trading concern in the borough, cater'ng for more than half the people of Stalybridge. He trusted members would rally round and try to make that year of their jubilee one of the best and most prosperous their society had known. He could not call those present old people ; he had noticed that day much energy amongst them ; but they would remember the time when working people had shop-books, and credit, not cash-trading, was the rule. Then came the co-operative movement, and instead of a shop book a member was asked to have a share book, with something to his or her credit. The co-operative movement had done a great deal in Stalybridge, and he hoped it would continue. He relied on the members present to maintain it, to uplift it, to bring it to an even better position for doing good than it had yet attained. He could assure them that the committee, on their part, would do their utmost.

TEA PARTY AND CONCERT FOR THE MEMBERS OF MILLBROOK AND HEYROD BRANCHES.

On the 20th March, 1909, tea was served to about 498 persons at the Town Hall, and Mr. J. Fawley presided at the concert held at the same place. He extended a hearty welcome to those present, expressing the pleasure the committee felt at seeing so many members there, taking their part in the jubilee celebrations. He called upon Mr. W. E. Dudley, of Runcorn, who said he would, as Mr. Fawley had promised, speak as one co-operator to another. He associated himself with the co-operative movement because he believed it was to the co-operative movement that they would have to look for the salvation of the worker. The history of the Stalybridge Society spoke volumes to him, and he would advise them to let no one come between them and their society. Some queer statements as to the aims and principles and effects of the movement were made by some persons. He would be delighted if that hall were occupied by such men, and if they would heckle him on the subject. The movement sought absolutely earnest, whole-hearted publicity. One object of that gathering was to create thought and reflection, and he believed his hearers would agree that thought and reflection in the hearts and minds and practice of the working classes of this country were a standing necessity. If they and he had many years ago thought more upon their own welfare and their own doings, their position would have been different that day. It had been said that ideas were like flowers weaving into garlands. Could they not find in their own minds a necessity for garlands in this life ? Were there not many homes into which such garlands had brought brightness ? Carlyle had said " a thinking man is the worst enemy that the prince of darkness can have." He would give them three points of a creed of Robert Owen, stated in 1834. The first was that the wants of all mankind should be met without slavery and without servitude. Robert Owen was not a man wanting to make a position for himself ; he was a man of affluence spending his life and money in improving the social condition of the working classes. He did not tell the workers at that time that labour was not required ; he said that labour was a blessing, but that slavery and servitude was a curse. Their chairman, Mr. Dudley continued, was concerned in the management of another institution that did much to reward labour as it should be rewarded. Not only did that society—the Co-operative Sundries Manufacturing Society—pay full wages, but it contributed bonus to labour in addition. That went to prove that where production was brought under the influence of co-operation, slavery and servitude were shunned. The workers shared in the profits they created, and sanitary conditions and everything desirable was brought in. The next point Owen wanted to raise was that all must be made intelligent, and all must be made charitable. Co-operators did not seek to take the workers outside their class, but they did help them to understand the problems of life better than they did before. Therefore they gave an opportunity of seeing things in a different light, and as the intelligence of the worker was raised, there would be a greater future for tha co-operative movement. In the third place, Owen wanted to say that co-operation must get rid of buying in the cheapest market and selling in the dearest. The producer in the outside world wanted to find when he went to market that everything he was about to put on the market was selling at the highest possible price. The consumer, when he went to market, desired that he should be able to purchase at the lowest possible price. The co-operative movement stepped in to level these interests. His hearers were both the producers and the consumers, and profit did not go to this or that section, but was divided equitably. Co-operators worked as a collective body, but observed the individuality of the collective system, and in proportion to that which they were prepared to contribute, whether in labour, capital, literary work, or management, so in proportion would be their reward. Henry Ward Beecher put it well when he said that to live aright and to assist human progress means this—that which you receive in seed must be handed on in blossom to the next generation, and that which you receive in blossom shall be handed on in fruit. Their pioneers in Stalybridge took the seed and handed on the blossom. They and he had that blossom; what were they doing to pass on the fruit? They should use every effort to build up those organisations of theirs, and then they could go on to the words of Dr. Norman Macleod :—

> Courage, brother, do not stumble,
> Though thy path be dark as night;
> There's a star to guide the humble—
> Trust in God and do the right.

An excellent programme was rendered by Mr. E. Spafford's Elite Concert Party, consisting of Miss Margaret Hadfield (soprano), Miss Helena Joy (contralto), Mr. John Collett (tenor), Mr. Harry Bray (baritone), and Mr. Frank Crawford (humorist), with Mr. Spafford himself as accompanist.

MOUNT PLEASANT BRANCH MEMBERS' GATHERING.

A tea party and concert for the members of Mount Pleasant Branch was held at the Town Hall on Saturday, 3rd April, 1909. Fully 600 people partook of tea, and an excellent programme was rendered by a concert party directed by Miss Pennington, of the Pennington Concert Agency, Longsight, Manchester.

The artistes were Madame Nellie Teggin (soprano), Miss Eva Sparkes (contralto), Mr. John Moran (tenor), Mr. G. H. Ditchburn (bass), Mr. Frank Crawford (entertainer), and Miss Pennington at the piano.

Mr. John Fawley took the chair, and introduced Mr. Charles Wright, manager of Manchester and Salford Society.

Mr. Wright congratulated the members on the great meeting in connection with the jubilee, and on the flourishing state of the society. It reminded him, he said, of an old man whom he heard at a party. He was a hundred years of age, and the jolliest old fellow at that gathering. Somebody said to him, " Why, John, you look as if you would live to be another hundred." "Well," he said, "why should I not ? I am a good deal stronger now than when I started the first hundred." The society was fifty, and he hoped it would go forward cheerfully and hopefully and unitedly towards the next half century. It had passed its infancy and early childhood, with the ailments incidental to childhood. Now they appeared in full manhood and full womanhood as members of a great and prosperous undertaking. The society he represented had been interested in the movement at Stalybridge right from the beginning, and he came that day from 18,000 members of Manchester and Salford to say to those of Stalybridge, " Go on and prosper." The Manchester and Salford pawnbrokers recently held their 100th anniversary, and they congratulated one another on the soundness and progressive character of the undertaking. He had no word of complaint against " uncle," who had perhaps helped occasionally someone to tide over a real difficulty, but there was an old proverb that " who goes a-borrowing goes a-sorrowing," and while he said nothing about visiting " uncle " for the purpose of getting a temporary loan, he did feel that there was a danger lest that going to " uncle " should crystallise into a habit, which would injure the moral fibre. Turning from the pawnbrokers to the store, he said the latter had something which no pawnbroker could show. His hearers were members of a great body numbering two-and-a-half millions of members, doing a trade of £103,000,000 a year, and dividing profits amounting to £11,000,000. During the past forty-five years the store movement in this country had earned for the members no less than 165 millions. Where would those profits have gone if not to members of co-operative societies ? They would have made a hundred millionaires ; but better a million people with £1 each in their pockets than one millionaire. Co-operators believed in better distribution of the world's wealth, and if that were achieved, there would not be such terrible stories of fellow men and women on the brink of starvation. There was talk about the greatness of our empire, and in many senses the empire was great ; but what was the good of an empire on which the sun never set to the man or woman who lived in a court where the sun never rose. We sang " Britons never shall be slaves." Were there not thousands of slaves in every city throughout the land ? Were there not crowds of helpless women and girls whose everyday life was a fight? He would give one or two instances of the pay to those women workers in Manchester. For making roses such as

CO-OPERATION IN STALYBRIDGE.

women wear in their hats, 3s. 6d. per gross was paid; for making parma violets and scarlet geraniums, 7d. per gross; for making shirts, five farthings each; and for making a pair of men's trousers, a woman was paid 5d. The women-folks should remember, when they were tempted to rush hither and thither, and to leave their own drapery store, that the average wage of the women workers of this country only worked out at $1\frac{1}{2}$d. to 2d. per hour. The workers did not want charity to help in such cases; they wanted better homes, better food, better wages, and more leisure to enjoy them. Surely the day of doom for the sweater and the sweating den was coming, and the day of hope for the toiler was at hand. Co-operation was trying to remedy that; it was trying to uplift people by paying a fair day's wage for a fair day's labour, by providing for the workers healthy and well-appointed workshops, such as the Stalybridge Society had in its tailoring department. It was trying to span with a golden bridge that great gulf which exists between the haves and the have-nots. He urged his hearers as co-operators to work heartily and unitedly for their own, for the growing good of this big and busy world. He believed the time was coming when co-operation would be more widely known and practised between man and man, and when it was, we should all understand that the roar of the blast-furnace was better than the roar of the cannon. It might be thought that this co-operation was going on in England only, but there were 146 journals in the world devoted to the popularising of co-operative principles, and co-operation was being widely practised abroad. As it took root abroad, people of different nationalities would look upon one another as brothers, and, as Mr. Seddon, M.P., said, we should know and feel that the gospel of co-operation was self-help, thrift, and international amity. He asked all to take with them, as they crossed the threshold of the jubilee into the next half-century, the message of "Peace on earth ; goodwill to men."

High Street and Cheetham Hill Road Members' Gathering.

There was a gathering of members from High Street and Cheetham Hill Road branches on Saturday, April 17th, 1909. Tea was served at Christ Church School to nearly 800 persons, and there was a concert at the Mechanics' Institution. The artistes were Miss Myra Dudley (soprano), Miss Annie Hargreaves (contralto), Mr. J. W. Cottrell (tenor), Mr. Samuel A. Moore (bass), Mr. Fred Ashcroft (humorous entertainer), and Mr. E. Spafford (accompanist).

Mr. George Hayhurst, of Accrington, a director of the Co-operative Wholesale Society, addressed the gathering. He was there, and he felt honoured thereby, to rejoice with them at their jubilee. He noticed that it was announced on the programme as a party for the younger members ; he looked at some of those before him, and thought—well, that they were getting on. (Laughter.) He had been trying to form a picture in his mind of the old man of that day and the same man as he appeared fifty years before. He was informed that a few of the co-operators of those early days remained in Stalybridge. All honour to them; the younger fellows before him owed a great deal to the grey hairs, and they should always respect them. But for the battles of their fathers, they would not enjoy the privileges they did. At a conference he had seen an old man of over seventy who heard another say, "Give me the good old days of fifty years ago." "Nay, nay, noan soa," said the old man; "I were livin' then, tha knows, an' I want noan o'th' old days; I have my tit-bit now." He was delighted that the old people had their pension of 5s. a week. (Hear, hear, and applause.) He was proud that the Stalybridge Society had that jubilee year beaten its record. Were they as good co-operators that day as those of fifty years ago? (A voice: "Better.") He was glad to hear that word "better." Those Stalybridge co-operators of fifty years ago were proud of their little shop, and if his hearers were as thorough as their pioneers, they would not go outside their own shops for anything. He reminded his audience of the words of the Rev. C. G. Lang, D.D., when Bishop of Stepney, at the Stratford Congress Exhibition in 1904 :—

> You won't forget, will you, those great ideals in the midst of which co-operation was born, when the working classes were banded together not only to raise their capital, but to raise their character. You should always keep those ideals before you, and maintain the honour of the goods you sell. Let it never be said of co-operative factories that they turn out shoddy articles. Let it never be said of a distributive store that it tried to make money by permitting the sale of goods which could not possibly be as cheap as represented unless there was sweating going on somewhere.

He had no patience, said Mr. Hayhurst, with the trade-unionist who went into the cheapest shop he could find. Every trade-unionist should be a co-operator, and every one ought to be true to his ideals. Trade union funds had been the means of keeping the wolf from the door, and from the Co-operative Wholesale Society alone there had been over £300,000 expended in relieving distress. He reminded his hearers that they were a part of that great organisation, which had a trade turnover of nearly £25,000,000 a year, and its own bank with a turnover of £100,000,000 a year. The power they possessed was power they should be proud of and stick to. If, as one member present had said, they were as good co-operators as those of fifty years ago, how was it that of a trade of £100,000,000 done in the movement, only £25,000,000 found its way to their own Wholesale? They could make it more. An old lady of over seventy had given him a motto. It was :—

> Whatever you are, be that;
> Whatever you do, be true;
> Straightforwardly act,
> Be honest, in fact,
> Be nobody else but you.

The co-operative movement had been built up to what it was in spite of opposition, in spite of boycotting; and, without legislation, if all men were true brothers, there could be brought about such a state of affairs as had never been dreamed of in the wisest man's philosophy. They had, in their own Wholesale Society, people working a 48 hours week, the men having a four-course dinner supplied them for 4d. and the girls a similar dinner for 3d. Those girls did not work in the clothes they went to and from the works in. Such were the conditions under which the people worked, and a good profit was made. Yet many of the mothers present did not, he was afraid, buy the biscuits made by themselves in those works. He had a message for the men, too, that they could get the best clothes cheap from their own works without any sweating. There was opened at Dunston-on-Tyne, the day before, a soap works that would turn out over 200 tons of soap a week, and when fully occupied 900 tons a week, without giving watches for coupons. They had five flour mills of their own. They were producing for themselves nearly £8,000,000 worth of goods every year. If they were as good co-operators as those of fifty years ago, Stalybridge Society would have a big increase that year. People said we should buy from our own. "Yes," concluded the speaker, "this society is your own, and be sure you buy from your own. Be true to one another, and success will attend every effort." (Applause.)

HUDDERSFIELD ROAD AND STOCKS BRANCHES' PARTY.

There was a gathering of the members of Huddersfield Road Branch, together with about a hundred of those of Stocks Branch, at the Town Hall, on Saturday, April 24th, 1909. Tea was served to 850 persons, and a concert was given by Miss Myra Dudley (soprano), Miss Annie Barker (contralto), Mr. Stanley Jenkinson (tenor), Mr. G. H. Ditchburn (bass), Mr. Fred Price (humorist), and Mr. Ernest Spafford (accompanist). Mr. John Fawley occupied the chair. He introduced Mr. William Lander, a director of the Co-operative

Wholesale Society, expressing a wish that everyone present would think about what Mr. Lander said. He was a man of vast experience in the movement, and there was no better to speak to co-operators on co-operation.

Mr. Lander said it would seem almost unkind, with such a fine programme before them, to ask them to listen to a long address. It was fitting, however, on such occasions that something should be said in reference to the co-operative movement. That meeting was one of a series at which they were rejoicing over the attainment of their jubilee. He was delighted to renew his acquaintance with Stalybridge co-operators for the purpose of joining with them in rejoicing that they had accomplished such an event and had made such remarkable progress during the fifty years of their existence as a society. He gathered from figures supplied to him by their secretary that since they commenced they had done a trade of about £3,000,000, and, as a result of their activity, had had returned to them something like £430,000 dividend and interest. Those were figures and facts about which they should rejoice, for they spoke volumes for their appreciation of the advantages that co-operation conferred on them in their own society, and proved to them the value of combination for the improvement of the people. Co-operation was a power and an influence for good in the State, judging it by what it had done not only in that town, but throughout the length and breadth of the United Kingdom, indeed almost throughout the civilised world. Fifty years was an important period in the history of the individual, the institution, or the nation. Perhaps some of them had seen the realisation of fifty years of married life and a golden wedding. The uniting of two individuals represented in miniature the larger coming together for the purpose of helping one another. Fifty years ago their pioneers in Stalybridge, and those of many other societies, joined together to improve the lives, to better the condition of the people, in a word, to help one another. That was the basis of co-operation, and it was a noble ideal that the movement always had before it. To him co-operation was a profoundly sacred thing. Social reform was, or ought to be, in the heart and mind of every true citizen of this great empire, and co-operation was practical voluntary social reform, a joining together for self-help and self-improvement, and therefore true, practical, every-day Christianity. (Hear, hear, and applause.) They in Stalybridge had travelled fifty years, the movement had travelled about sixty-five, and there were immense figures showing success all along the line. Great difficulties had been encountered, but unity of purpose, one-ness of heart, and determination had brought about the great result seen that day. Their society in Stalybridge had been one of the blessings of their town. Its influence on the distribution of the wealth of the town had made for the domestic happiness of the people. Would anyone tell him that the homes in Stalybridge were not that day better because of co-operation? Fifty years ago those homes were unsatisfactory, but they had been greatly improved, and that improvement had been brought about by the spirit of combination. He believed that the individual system of ruling commercial life was played out, and that it must be ruled on collective lines in the future. He was connected with a great institution—the Co-operative Wholesale Society—which would in about five years be celebrating its jubilee. It was doing a trade as merchant and manufacturer of £25,000,000, and joining the nations of the world together co-operatively. What it had done was only a tittle of what he hoped it would do; there was a greater work in front of it. Distribution had been a great and grand work, but the organising of industry on collective lines was a greater work still. Industrialism was still unsatisfactory. There were many places where the workers ought to have shorter hours, and better conditions in which to work, and he believed the people could get both if they combined and were determined. He thought the greatest difficulty before the country was, not the building of "Dreadnoughts" and the fighting of foreign nations, but the social evils of the time. He believed every industry could have a 48 hours week; co-operation had done it and was doing it, and if the workers were determined the principle could be extended. He had the honour to preside over the productive works of the great Wholesale Society, which employed 11,000 people in production alone, and which paid no man less than 24s. a week. He did not boast of that 24s.; it was not enough, but it was a great advance on the conditions once existing, and they could get it best by combining in co-operation. There was not another factory in this country where females were employed making shirts, working 46 hours a week, and getting an average wage of from 19s. to 20s. for it. On the other hand, there were poor women working in Ancoats that day making shirts, and ladies' blouses, too, in their own houses, finding their own thread and machines and gas, and getting 9d. a dozen for making shirts and 1s. 1½d. a dozen for making ladies' blouses. It was a scandal, and the way out was through co-operation. For what the co-operative movement had done and was doing for them in Stalybridge, he urged them to take a deeper interest in it as a social reforming influence for the generations yet to come. They should hold to their store, and support those works in which good conditions existed, in order that they might be extended. Mr. Lander concluded: "Learn more about the movement, practice its principles more, try to usher in a better time for the present generation, and leave a glorious heritage for those to come, as our forefathers have for us." (Loud applause.)

KAY STREET AND STOCKS BRANCHES' GATHERING.

A gathering of the members of Kay Street and Stocks branches was held at the Town Hall on Saturday, May 1st, 1909. Tea was served to 700 persons, and there was a concert by Miss Bessie Blackburn (soprano), Miss Annie Hargreaves (contralto), Mr. Albert J. Holt (tenor), Mr. Arthur Weber (bass), Mr. John Drake (Yorkshire humorist), and Mr. Ernest Spafford (accompanist.)

Mr. J. Taylor, one of the staff of the Co-operative Wholesale Society at Balloon Street, addressed the audience. He said he felt very much like a culprit to have to intervene between those present and the excellent programme they had before them. If they would give him their patience, however, he would not long take their attention. He was reminded of the woman who sought a separation order. When asked by the judge why she wanted a separation, she said it was because he had never spoken to her for a month. The husband was asked if that were so, and why, and he replied, " Please, sir, I didn't want to interrupt her." Even if they cried " Votes for women," he had no friends in the Government, and he would advise them to let him have the few minutes at his disposal. They had seen fit that night to honour one of the workers, and he thought they were like the lady controlling the use of her fire-irons. Let any mere man attempt to poke the fire with the beautiful irons of the sitting-room, and he would be told " No ! there is a little common poker round the corner for that." He was a little common poker. They owed much to the starters of the co-operative movement, who by their wise provision for depreciation, and by their setting aside of reserve funds, had made it possible for the co-operators of that later time to step forward more bravely. The movement was only fourteen or fifteen years old when they started in Stalybridge, and the people were struggling against such things as the Corn Laws. They commenced the co-operative movement with the object of getting the profits from distribution. There were many ladies present, and he was glad of it. Whilst the men were earning 80 per cent of the wages, the women were earning 20 per cent. On the other hand, whilst the women were spending 75 per cent, the men were content with the remaining 25 per cent. He was quite willing to let the husband be the prime

CO-OPERATION IN STALYBRIDGE. 267

minister, but the wife should be the chancellor of the exchequer. A wife must go where she could get the best, and a pound's worth must not cost her twenty-one shillings. Where a person looked for a shop showing the lowest prices, it was a case of the biter bit. If they looked around in their own town they would see that there were nine or ten times too many shops in which small businesses were conducted. The co-operative movement concentrated and economised, and it had solved the problem of distribution. If a number of those engaged in shopkeeping could be employed in more successful methods of producing something, a useful work would have been accomplished. They as co-operators had works of their own, turning out goods of absolute purity, under proper conditions, and without the expenditure of immense sums in advertising. Hence they were economising when they purchased those goods. He had seen it stated in one of the newspapers of a day or two before that skirts were made by women for 1s. 9d. a dozen, and that leaves for prayer-books and bibles were being folded at a price that would not keep body and soul together. They could be quite sure that goods made in their own co-operative works were produced under proper conditions. They had the only biscuit factory working an eight hours day, and the biscuit factory was not an isolated example. They in Stalybridge were one of 1,418 societies. Truly, as Lord Rosebery had said, the great principle of the union of interests in the co-operative movement constituted a state within a state. If they went to their stores and did not get what they wanted, let them tell, not the neighbourhood, but the management; or, in the words of others, "If we please you, tell others; if we don't, tell us." The business was theirs, and he hoped that in the days to come even brighter and better things could be said of it because they had supported it. A young man had wanted to see his young lady. He was in a difficulty, because she had retired. He went beneath her window and called out " fire ! " and when a night-capped head appeared at the window and asked " where ? " he replied " here." They required more fire. They were rejoicing on having attained their jubilee. He trusted they would hand on to those who would come after a glorious heritage of co-operation unsullied, realising that they were there not so much to jubilate about the past, but to seek the best for the future.

Gathering of the Members of Central and Stocks Branch.

On Saturday, May 8th, 1909, tea was served to 744 persons at the Town Hall. Again Mr. Ernest Spafford, of Hooley Hill, brought a concert party, and again a delightful evening's entertainment was the result. The artistes were Miss Myra Dudley (soprano), Miss Annie Hargreaves (contralto), Mr. A. J. Holt (tenor), Mr. G. H. Ditchburn (bass), Mr. Frank Crawford (humorist), and Mr. E. Spafford (accompanist). After Miss Dudley's first song, Mr. John Fawley (chairman) said the talented artiste they had just heard came from Crewe; Mr. Crawford, the clever humorous entertainer, came from Crewe; and the next item on the programme was a brief address by Mr. Miles Parkes, who came from Crewe. They were certainly a very good crew. (Laughter.)

Mr. Parkes, a director of the Co-operative Wholesale Society, expressed the pleasure he felt in being present to rejoice with the members on the occasion of their society's jubilee. In the middle of the last century, he said, the working classes of this country were struggling for existence. Bread was dear, and flesh and blood were cheap; education was denied the working man, his hours of labour were many, and his wages at starvation rates. The working man was isolated and entirely at the mercy of the capitalist. Suffering under those conditions, the historic pioneers of Rochdale decided to strike a blow for freedom, and introduced a new scheme of social amelioration. To what great ends did small beginnings sometimes lead. The great movement with which they were proud to be identified was born of the seed of discontent in the soil of starvation, and it had by the magnitude of its operations so elevated the masses that an indelible imprint on the national history had been made. By the influence of the co-operative movement the working classes of the country had not only acquired for themselves millions of capital, but they had elevated their lives, brightened their prospects, and secured for themselves a position otherwise unattainable to them. He believed that the future of the working classes depended whether commerce was to be conducted on co-operative or competitive lines. Under the existing system of competition it was a case of every man for himself and the devil take the hindmost. The co-operative principle made for friendship, fellowship, and human brotherhood, and its ultimate triumph would mean the displacement of the spirit of cut-throat competition for the higher aims of associated service and concerted action. The co-operative movement was both sound in principle and beneficial in practice, because it aimed at the welfare of all. It sought to put out all that tended to enrich the few at the expense of the many. In the field of commerce, consumption, distribution, and production were, generally speaking, antagonistic, each prospering as it took advantage of the others. Hence such keen competition which, as Carlyle said, had rendered life, not a matter of mutual helpfulness, but rather of social war and mutual hostility. The co-operative idea taught that persons engaged in commercial transactions were not rivals, but friends. As Ruskin put it, it was an exchange among friends whereby there should be no undue advantage on either side, but rather an equal advantage on both sides. The more that spirit could be infused into trade and commerce, the nearer should we approach that time

> When man to man the world o'er
> Shall brothers be and a' that.

By our system of co-operation we were seeking to bring the consumer into direct contact with the producer, and thus the consumer was gradually regulating the conditions under which his goods were produced and sold, and helping to bring together the atoms of society to a state in which each shall seek his own in all men's good, and all men work together in noble brotherhood. He likened co-operation to a bridge, at one end of which there was superabundance and at the other penury. Thousands of thrifty toilers were passing, tapping for themselves those great reservoirs of wealth, and establishing a new system of industrial peace more in harmony with justice and with sound national policy. The tendency of co-operative operations was to bring about a diminution of poverty by removing inequalities. Under a national system of co-operation we should have fewer millionaires, fewer people with immense fortunes, but a more contented peasantry and artisan people, and, after all, a thrifty, intelligent, sober democracy was the backbone of this or any country. The Stalybridge Society was distributing among the working people of the town no less than £20,000 per annum. Just imagine some wealthy person making such a gift year after year. His portrait would be in every home, and a statue would be erected to perpetuate his memory. Was it not better and nobler for the working classes, by this system of associated effort, to get for themselves those large sums without being dependent on anyone? In ten years the movement had accumulated for the workers no less a sum than £100,000,000 which would otherwise have gone to people already wealthy. But money was of value only so far as it was usefully employed. He supposed there was no question that so greatly agitated the minds of the working classes and of social reformers as that of the industrial problem, and he contended that if the great labour problem was to be solved, it would be by the application of the principles of co-operation. Much of the confusion of the working world sprang from the fact that capitalists had possession of the implements of labour. The man who owned those implements had only to say to the man at the wheel, "hands off," and he was thrown out of employment. Co-operators wanted to accumulate their capital in order that they might secure for themselves their implements of labour. The more manufactures they could enter into, the better provision they could make for old age, and the greater facilities they would have for doing away with the workhouse and the scandal of the pauper's grave. They could only succeed in raising the standard of living to the working classes in proportion to the support the members gave to their societies. He remembered a story of a newly-married couple who purchased a perambulator. The young wife placed her first-born in it and they started for home. People smiled. The husband walked round the carriage, and found on it a ticket bearing the words: "Our own make; may be had at the stores, 18s. 6d. each." The moral was, when they went to the stores to make their purchases they should ask for "our own make." That would be a valuable contribution on their part to the desired result. Let them not be tempted away by any bait, however alluring, and they would be helping to make their society even more successful in the future than in the past. Thus would their efforts be blended in trying to make this movement a still greater boon and blessing to the workers of the country.

> What might be done if men were wise,
>   What noble deeds, my suffering brother,
> Did men unite in love and right,
>   And cease their hate of one another.

Oppression's heart would be imbued
With kindling drops of loving kindness,
And knowledge pour from shore to shore,
Light up the eyes of human blindness.

The meanest wretch that ever trod,
The lowest sunk in grief and sorrow,
Might stand erect in self-respect
And share this teeming world to-morrow.

What might be done? This might be done,
And more than this, my suffering brother,
More than the heart e'er said or sung,
If men were wise and loved each other.

The concert was then proceeded with, and item after item was encored. Soprano, contralto, tenor, and bass, all had their meed of praise, and the humorous selections of Mr. Crawford, and the humorous duets of Miss Dudley and Mr. Crawford, were greatly enjoyed. After the National Anthem, with which the programme concluded, there was another spontaneous outburst of applause.

Exhibition.

An exhibition of co-operative productions and work in progress, organised by the Co-operative Wholesale Society Limited, and under the direction of Mr. H. Gill, of the Wholesale Society, was opened at the Town Hall, on Saturday, 15th May, 1909, and continued until Wednesday, the 19th, inclusive.

Mr. John Fawley presided. He announced that letters of regret for their unavoidable absence had been received from the Reverends T. H. Sheriff, C. Sutcliffe, T. M. Oldfield, C. Rushby, and H. Hawley. Some of them expected to visit the exhibition before it was closed. That exhibition had been arranged as one form in which the jubilee should be celebrated, just to show the people something of what was being produced within their own movement. Production as a sphere of co-operative activity was very important, and it was insufficiently understood by the general body of members. Some thought that whenever they made a purchase at one of the society's stores they were buying co-operative goods, but that was not always the case, and it should be the duty and pleasure of every manager and assistant to bring prominently before the members the goods made by co-operators, for co-operators, with co-operative capital. Those goods were made in well-built, well-ventilated works, from pure, unadulterated materials. The sanitary conditions were perfect, the best wages paid, and the workers were happy and contented without driving. What a contrast to the conditions existing in some of the sweating dens of this country, where men and women were employed very long hours at starvation rates, working, living, cooking their food, ay! even sleeping in the same room. The whole life of such people was crushed out of them by the sweater, and they ultimately gave up the struggle and ceased to look for anything better. How were those people to lift themselves to something higher? It was to counteract such conditions that co-operative manufactories were established, and he trusted the exhibition would have the effect of inducing more of the members of Stalybridge Society to ask for their own productions.

Mr. T. E. Moorhouse, a director of the Co-operative Wholesale Society Limited, said it gave him great pleasure to be present to rejoice in the jubilee of the Stalybridge Society. When, fifty years ago, the pioneers of the movement in the town put their heads together for the formation of a co-operative society, the condition of the working classes throughout Great Britain was anything but rosy, and there could be no doubt that it was owing to the depressed conditions under which many then lived that the idea of co-operation took root, and that so many societies were organised in that part of the country about the same time. Coming as he did from a neighbouring village— Delph—where co-operation had been in existence about the same number of years, he could assure them that there was in the history of those organisations very much that was interesting. That exhibition was to show what the people could do for themselves. He believed in self-help rather than too much borrowed help. Co-operation meant self-help, and the productive side of the movement was one of the most hopeful. He had received, a few days before, the annual return of the Co-operative Union, which would be open to discussion by some 1,600 delegates at the Newcastle Congress in Whit-week, and he found that the co-operative trade of Great Britain for the year 1908 amounted to more than £107,000,000, an increase over the previous year of £1,832,000, and when they considered that the year 1907 was one of the greatest years for commercial boom that Great Britain had known, and when they remembered the terrible commercial depression existing during the greater part of 1908, he thought they would realise that co-operation had more than held its own. He thought the imports and exports of Great Britain in 1908 were something like £114,000,000 less than the previous year, and that being so, it was a great triumph for the co-operative movement to have a substantial increase. They were more particularly concerned that afternoon with productive co-operation. He had attended the sweating exhibition held in Manchester some two or three years before. It was an opportunity for people to see for themselves, in the kind of goods produced, a miniature reflection of the conditions under which people laboured and under under which the goods were produced. As co-operators, they believed that those who toiled from Monday morning to Saturday noon were the people who ought to have the best which the earth could produce, and who ought to work under the best possible conditions. It was with that ideal that co-operative production had its inception, and they had been trying to work to that ideal ever since. When the twenty-eight pioneers of Rochdale met to form their society, it was stated in an introduction to their rules that their object was to obtain control, not only of the means of distribution, but also of the means of production, and that was still the aim of the movement. They had before them that day just a hint of what was being done by the Co-operative Wholesale Society. The Wholesale Society had a total turnover last year of close upon £25,000,000. It had some sixty co-operative factories or productive workshops, and during the year ended December, 1908, had put out from those workshops goods to the value of £5,750,000. It might not be generally known, but they were the largest corn millers in the United Kingdom, they had five shoe factories employing 4,000

CO-OPERATION IN STALYBRIDGE. 277

to 5,000 hands, a woollen mill at Batley, cocoa works at Luton, jam works at Middleton, biscuit works at Crumpsall, soap works at Irlam, Silvertown, and Dunston-on-Tyne. Those were just a few of the industries in which the Wholesale Society engaged. In Ireland they ran seventy to eighty creameries, where butter was made under the best possible conditions. The turnover in butter alone was more than £4,500,000 during 1908. Nearly £3,000,000 value was brought from Denmark, and if the producers would take a lesson from Denmark, agriculture in Great Britain would be in a better position. When he read that we were importing food to the value of over £7,000,000 per annum, he thought a great quantity could be produced in our own land had we more equitable conditions, more reasonable landlords, and co-operation among the people. Those were the things co-operators were aspiring for, and by means of exhibitions such as the one to be opened there that day, the people could realise the possibilities in the direction of doing for themselves. They could go on from victory to victory toward the time when sweating dens would be unknown, and every working man's home would be a paradise on earth. (Applause.)

Mr. J. F. Cheetham, M.P., said it was a pleasure to be present on an occasion of so much local interest. They were there that afternoon for a purpose far transcending the sphere of party political controversies. After the admirable speeches from experts just listened to, he felt it would be presumption on his part to address at great length the instructed audience before him. The vast importance of co-operation as a dominant factor in the social progress of the community had been recognised by eminent men in every department of our national life, by our most eminent thinkers in economics, and by politicians of all parties. (Hear, hear.) He would like to cull from some leaflets which had been sent to him along with the programme, one or two of the opinions of such men. The greatest of Liberal statesmen, Mr. Gladstone, had said, "There has not been a better thing done in this country, in my opinion, than the establishment of co-operation, such as the successful co-operation of which Lancashire deserves the principal credit." Another, of very different political views, Lord Derby, said, "It is not in the language of idle flattery, but as the expression of a deliberate and sincere conviction, that I begin by telling you that the subject which brings this Congress together is, in my judgment, more important as regards the future of England than nine-tenths of those discussed in Parliament, and around which political controversy gathers." With those two statesmen he entirely agreed. (Applause.) It was a matter of surprise to him that Parliament, which devoted so much time to legislation affecting the conflicting interests of labour and capital upon their present basis, should be doing so little to pursue the practical application of co-operation in our industries, that practical application through which alone, he believed, could be brought about a permanent and satisfactory solution of what was perhaps the most difficult problem of the day. He would not take up more of their time by stating the opinions of such statesmen as Lord Shaftesbury, of economists such as Cairnes, John Stuart Mill, and others. He had had some conversation with a friend of his in the House of Commons, Mr. H. Vivian, M.P., who had put into his hands a paper showing the great progress made by co-operation in recent years, especially distributive co-operation. Whilst the number of members of co-operative societies in 1890 was a little over a million, in 1908 they had reached 2,400,000. Their holding in shares had increased from £10,600,000 to £30,000,000, and their trade profit had jumped from £3,760,000 to £10,750,000 in the same period. The results of productive co-operation, with which they were mainly concerned that day, did not compare with those of distribution. There were two forms of distributive co-operation, that form with which they were concerned that day, and co-partnership. Some statistics of the results of the productive departments of the English Wholesale Society had been given them. He found that there had been a four-fold growth during the years 1890 to 1908, and that seemed a very satisfactory growth. Much greater encouragement should be given to productive co-operation, and he looked forward to the time when many of our great industries would be organised on the co-operative principle, for during the last thirty or forty years his conviction had been that it was only by organising our industries that we could bring about a sure industrial peace, and do away with the conflicts between labour and capital on their present footing. (Applause.) They were then suffering from a trouble in the cotton industry which would not have occurred, he thought, if the trade had been organised on the co-operative principle. He attached great importance to the co-operative principle in our industrial system. He had often wondered whether it might be hoped, now that trade-unionism had so completely organised its forces, and societies had attained to such a full measure of freedom of action, if they would turn their attention to promote the principle of co-operation in various industries. They had control of large means, and he hoped they would throw themselves heartily into that movement and bring their best influence to bear upon what he considered as perhaps the most important social question of the day. They sometimes heard alarmist expressions of the danger of co-operation encroaching upon individual enterprise. He confessed that in those matters he was very much an individualist. He believed there was scarcely one of our great industries which had not been originated by individual enterprise and skill and energy; but there was really no conflict, or ought not to be, between the two principles. It was, he believed, to the action and reaction of individualism and co-operation that we must look for the development of our great industrial system. We could not afford to do without either, but individual effort should be brought to bear upon co-operation. Productive co-operation especially should have attention, and he trusted that exhibition would show them the possibilities of productive activity. He thought there was great scope for it, and he cordially re-echoed the sentiment of the chairman, that increasing interest would be taken by the community in that most important question, and that there would be found springing up co-operative societies devoted to production. They would, he believed, tend very largely to diminish the risk of industrial strife; they were in themselves effectual means of education, and, above all, they tended to produce so much public spirit amongst those who were interested as members. The amount of interest taken in public questions by the leaders in those societies, and the contributions by the societies to the promotion of education and other good objects were remarkable, and the best proof, he thought, of the moral effect of co-operation. He hoped the exhibition would conduce to a fuller knowledge and wider interest in productive co-operation, and that in that district and others there would be seen a movement largely developed in a direction which he was sure would be for the advancement and progress of the community, not merely in purely material matters, but in all the higher social questions. He expressed the pleasure he felt in being amongst the constituents he had the honour to represent, and a hope that circumstances beyond his control would no longer prevent his coming amongst them. He wished all success and prosperity to the exhibition and to the cause it was desired to advance. (Applause.)

Mr. Councillor Bottomley moved a vote of thanks to Mr. Cheetham and Mr. Moorhouse for the excellent addresses they had given. All knew the deep interest Mr. Cheetham took in the borough, and many of them knew of the important office held by Mr. Moorhouse as a director of the Co-operative Wholesale Society. He would like to give Mr. Moorhouse a hint. If they extended the operations of the Wholesale Society, they might remember that there were eligible sites in Stalybridge. He would be very pleased indeed to see some of the works in the borough.

282   CO-OPERATION IN STALYBRIDGE.

Mr. W. Wardle, J.P., seconded the vote of thanks, and Mr. Fawley asked Mr. Cheetham to accept a specially bound copy of the Co-operative Wholesale Societies' Annual.

Mr. Cheetham said he must express his grateful appreciation of the kindly feeling shown. He hoped that, as his friend Mr. Bottomley had said, the societies might turn to account some portion of the unoccupied land of the borough, which they knew was to be brought under taxation. (Laughter.) He thanked the society most heartily for the gift of the beautiful volume just handed to him. He would study it with much interest, and treasure it as a proof of good feeling towards him by so influential a body of his fellow-townsmen.

In acknowledging the vote of thanks, Mr. Moorhouse said he was not in a position to make any promise. He would, however, report to his colleagues that Stalybridge had had a very successful opening of the exhibition, and that the town had further ambition in the direction of co-operative production. Perhaps, when the time came for new works, they would get a look in.

After the opening, tea was served to delegates from neighbouring societies and other visitors in the society's hall. A vote of thanks to the society for the manner in which the company had been entertained was moved by Mr. J. R. Smith (president of the Co-operative Sundries Manufacturing Society, Droylsden), seconded by Mr. James Kershaw (president of Rochdale Pioneers' Society), supported by Mr. T. E. Moorhouse, and acknowledged by Mr. John Fawley.

The Children's Day.

As the annual soirée or concert was merged in the jubilee proceedings, so did the ninth annual children's gala, held June 12th, become a part of the celebration. The weather was delightful, and the day a most enjoyable one, not only to the children, but to adults as well. Children to the number of 3,010 had previously obtained free tickets entitling them to a bun and milk and a souvenir mug each. Shortly after half-past one they commenced to move in procession from the market ground, accompanied by the Ancient Shepherds' Reed Band and the Stalybridge Borough Brass Band. At the head was a trap driven by Mr. David Warren, the horsekeeper. Then came ten decorated lorries belonging to the Stalybridge and other societies. Those of Stalybridge were driven by Messrs. J. Bullock, T. H. Daniels, J. Clements, J. Healey, O. Wardle, H. Norton, and C. Hodge, all of whom had contributed to the effectiveness of the display by the careful grooming of their horses and attention to the lorries. The first lorry carried a number of lambs, representing the butchering department, whilst drapery was represented by a neat and attractive arrangement of curtains, rugs, &c. Another lorry held a display of cocoas, chocolates, &c., from the Luton Works of the Wholesale Society, arranged to depict a motor car, and as the procession moved the wheels of the car revolved. The Wholesale Society's Sun and Star Flour Mills were represented by a windmill composed of boxes of flour. Following this was a lorry from the Crumpsall Biscuit Works and another with a display of health salt, baking powder, sweets,

&c., in enormous tins. Ashton Society had two lorries there ; the first was very imposing, set out with butter, bacon, hams, and Star flour ; and the second carried a very smartly arranged suite of furniture. Hyde Society was represented by an equally smart show of furniture on an exquisitely decorated lorry. The Co-operative Sundries Society, of Droylsden, had a display of the unrivalled "Beehive" specialities ; Higher Hurst Society one of soaps from the Irlam Works of the Wholesale Society ; and Hurst Brook Society brought up the rear with another display of C.W.S. products with a decorated lifeboat in the centre. Following the conveyances came the children, girls first, carrying numerous union jacks bearing mottoes. The route taken was Corporation Street, Melbourne Street, Market Street, Water Street, Caroline Street, Bridge Street, Stanley Square, High Street, Grosvenor Street, Acres Lane, and Mottram Road, to a field at Bower Fold. At the field sports were held and there were several other attractions, the entertainments including Punch with performing dog, ventriloquism, mimicry, marionettes, a knockabout stilt performer introducing a giant woman, and clown with giant football. Marquees had been erected by Messrs. Illingworth Brothers, and in one of these refreshments were served. Amongst others present were about 40 children from the workhouse, who took part in the sports and other attractions. Prizes were offered to and eagerly competed for by the children, and there were also prizes for the horses and turnouts.

Conclusion of Jubilee Celebration.

The employés' day out was, with the exception of the publication of the history, the final item in the jubilee programme. Two places were selected, 37 members of the staff giving in their names for Worksop and the Dukeries, and the remainder, about 80 in number, for Chester.

The teas and concerts were attended altogether by 5,030 persons; it was estimated that the exhibition was visited by 20,000, and the gala by some thousands in addition to the children who had obtained tickets.

Conclusion.

It has been shown that we came into existence as a society in a very small way, but in the hands of careful nurses. When our pioneers sought the advice of those of Rochdale in 1859, our Rochdale friends wrote, through Mr. William Cooper, himself undoubtedly a careful man, that they thought business could be commenced in Stalybridge earlier than had been proposed; but our stalwarts made sure of their position, and when they did start it was in no haphazard manner.

Some of those pioneers, such as Mr. John Bramall, Mr. W. Evans, and Mr. Hugh Wilson, we still have with us. In the troublous times of the early 'sixties members went to Mr. Bramall saying they were sure the society would go down, and asking if he intended to withdraw. His reply was No! I will not withdraw; I will buy your shares. In some cases he did take over the shares; in others his confidence had the effect of reassuring doubtful ones, and so they went on, feeling that—

> If the thing's to be won there's nought to be done
> But just keeping pegging away.

They met with opposition. So does every good cause when misunderstood. It was stated in a recent issue of a trade paper that Turkey was going ahead. One of the causes of its lagging behind, it was said, was that Turkish officialdom could not distinguish between dynamo and dynamite. The result was the prohibition of electric tramways. But Turkey is getting its tramways.

On the foundation laid by such staunch members has been raised the present superstructure. This jubilee year we are stronger than at any other time in our history. May we go on. remembering, with Pope, that—

> All are but parts of one stupendous whole,

and, as Abraham Lincoln pleaded,

> With malice toward none; with charity for all; with firmness in the right, as God gives us to see the right, let us strive to finish the work we are in.

APPENDIX.

PAST AND PRESENT OFFICERS.

CHAIRMEN AND PRESIDENTS, AND YEARS FIRST ELECTED.

Johanan Booth	1859	John Milligan	1872
James Heywood	1859	John Ridgway	1872
John France	1859	John Bennett	1873
Joseph Edgar	1859	Allen Heppenstall	1873
Thomas Ellis	1860	John Shaw	1873
Joseph Woolhouse	1860	John Heap	1873
Alexander Maxwell	1860	Augustus Ball	1873
Daniel Woolley	1860	Joseph Britnor	1873
Charles Gaskell	1860	John Buckley	1874
James Cook	1860	James Cheetham	1874
Joseph Swift	1865	John Street	1875
Matthew Hutchinson	1865	William Hall	1878
Marshall Ashworth	1865	James McCall	1880
John Hampshire	1865	Samuel Sidebottom	1881
John Thorp	1865	F. B. Wilde	1882
John Hackett	1865	Wright Hadfield	1885
William Morrison	1865	Thomas Knott	1888
Peter Unsworth	1865	Thomas Wood	1890
Joshua Hill	1865	Thomas Shepley	1893
Amos Mellor	1866	James Senior	1894
John Bamford	1866	John Fawley	1894
Joseph Kay	1866	John T. Bate	1895
Robert Whittle	1866	Allen Hopwood	1897
Hugh Kenworthy	1867	Thomas Beard	1897
Robert Bullock	1867	Samuel Knight	1897
George Woodhead	1867	William Wardle	1897
John Lawton	1868	William Shaw	1898
Joseph Cottrell	1868	Joseph Carter	1898
John Flitcroft	1869	George R. Patten	1898
William J. Chadwick	1870	E. P. Owens	1902
Aaron Warhurst	1871		

COMMITTEE.

Past and Present, and Year First Elected.

Name	Year	Name	Year
Allen, Joseph	1859	Heywood, James	1859
Allen, John	1894	Heppenstall, Allen	1873
Allsop, Joshua	1862	Heap, John	1873
Ashworth, Marshall	1865	Hill, Joshua	1865
Ashton, Ashton	1883	Hopwood, Allen	1895
Bamford, John	1859	Hutchinson, Matthew	1859
Blacker, Jonathan	1859	Hurst, Frank	1903
Ball, Augustus	1873	Jackson, Ambrose	1859
Bate, John T.	1894	Jones, Charles	1859
Bailey, James	1899	Kay, George	1859
Barnett, Thomas W.	1900	Kay, Joseph	1866
Bennett, John	1873	Kenworthy, Hugh	1866
Beard, Thomas	1895	Kenyon, William H.	1895
Britnor, Joseph	1873	Kinsey, Joseph	1862
Britain, George	1885	Knight, Samuel	1889
Booth, Johanan	1859	Knott, Thomas	1884
Booth, Squire	1900	Lawton, Robert	1865
Bullock, Robert	1859	Lawton, Ralph	1865
Buckley, John	1874	Lawton, John	1868
Chadwick, William J.	1870	Lawton, Hugh	1907
Carter, Joseph	1893	Maxwell, Alexander	1859
Cheetham, James	1874	McCall, James	1879
Cobham, Robert	1860	Mellor, Amos	1866
Cottrell, Joseph	1868	Milligan, John	1872
Cooke, William	1880	Morrison, William	1865
Cooper, Albert	1907	Norris, John	1893
Dickin, Albert E.	1908	Owens, William	1887
Dunne, William	1909	Owens, Edward P.	1898
Edgar, Joseph	1859	Patten, George R.	1897
Ellis, Thomas	1859	Porter, John Langford	1859
France, John	1859	Ridgway, John	1859
Fawley, John	1893	Roberts, William	1862
Flitcroft, John	1869	Rushton, George	1862
Frith, James	1875	Shaw, John	1873
Gaskell, Charles	1859	Shaw, Thomas	1881
Haynes, William	1859	Shaw, William	1896
Harrison, William	1860	Street, John	1875
Hampshire, John	1865	Shepley, Thomas	1887
Hackett, John	1865	Senior, James	1893
Hall, William	1876	Swift, Joseph	1859
Hadfield, Wright	1882	Stringer, David	1862
Haigh, James N.	1902	Sidebottom, Samuel	1879
Hanson, Richard	1906	Stubbs, Robert	1903

APPENDIX. 289

COMMITTEE—continued.

Thorpe, John	1859	Wilde, F. B.	1881
Thornley, Luke	1862	Wilkinson, Alfred	1905
Turner, Edward	1904	Woolley, Daniel	1859
Unsworth, Peter	1865	Woodhead, George	1867
Warhurst, Aaron	1871	Woolhouse, Joseph	1859
Wardle, William	1896	Wood, Samuel B.	1878
Whittle, Robert	1866	Wood, Thomas	1886
Wild, Levi	1862		

SECRETARIES.

Thomas Baxter	1859	Seth Charlesworth	1874
Samuel Hadfield	1862	James R. Jackson	1880
Joseph Greenwood	1865	James H. Hinchliffe	1894
Philip H. Robinson	1873		

TREASURERS.

Johanan Booth	1859	J. H. Hinchliffe	1893
James Lawton	1862	William Thompson	1894
John Ridgway	1868	Albert E. Jackson	1905
J. B. W. Buckley	1885	Edwin Wright	1907
William Backhurst	1888		

AUDITORS.

Alexander Maxwell	1859	George Cheetham	1870
Joshua Allsop	1859	John Jackson	1871
Bradburn Cocker	1860	John Heap	1873
George Hodgkinson	1862	*Samuel Hall	1886
James Carter	1862	Albert Bates	1886
W. Moores	1863	William Moss	1887
N. Moss	1863	W. H. Barker	1887
Isaac Bardsley	1865	George H. Whalley	1889
Thomas Hodson	1866	*Daniel Holt	1892
G. Thewlis	1870		

SOLICITORS.

Noah Buckley 1859
*Fred Thompson, LL.B. (Buckley, Miller,
    and Thompson) 1903
        * Present time.

APPENDIX.

MANAGERS.

James Hyde	1859	P. H. Robinson	1873
Henry Rowbottom..left	1864	F. R. Beeley	1874
Mr. Watson	1864	J. Mellor	1876
Joseph Greenwood	1866	J. B. Mason	1895

GROCERY CENTRAL AND BRANCH MANAGERS.
PRESENT TIME.

J. H. Milligan.	S. Smalley.
E. Lees.	F. Robinson.
H. Dawson.	H. Austerberry.
H. Sheffield.	G. Guthrie.
S. E. Whitlock.	

FIRST COUNTERMEN,
AND SOME OTHERS OF LONG SERVICE.
GROCERY.

William Simpson	1894	John Poole	1899
James Lawton	1895	George Lawton	1900
D. Woolley	1897	S. Eyre	1900
Thomas Horrocks	1898	F. Fielding	1901

DRAPERY.
P. J. Leigh 1908

BOOTS.
J. B. Senior 1906

TAILORING.
J. Walmsley.......................... 1904

BUTCHERING.

F. McKinlay	1889	Percy Howard	1900
James Norton	1894	Stanley Howard	1902
E. Clough	1895	Walter Eastwood	1905
Walter Holt	1899	Stanley Oakes ..1905 and 1908	

DEPARTMENT MANAGERS.
PRESENT TIME.

Check Office A. Shaw.	Boots ..... J. H. Austerberry.
Drapery.... T. Faulkner.	Butchering . Arthur Allen.
Dressmaking Miss S. Holt.	Coal .... Geo. Wilkinson.
Millinery ... Miss Firth.	Horsekeeper David Warren.
Tailoring .. J. Green.	

NUMBER OF MEMBERS AND SALES AT DIFFERENT PERIODS.

	Members.	Sales.
		£
November, 1859	139	..
First week in Water Street	..	84
January Quarter, 1860	..	1,132
1860	800	..
1861	2,000	42,114
July Quarter, 1862	..	6,930
October Quarter, 1862	..	5,411
September Quarter, 1863	..	3,476
December Quarter, 1863	..	3,605
December Quarter, 1864	..	2,208
March Quarter, 1865	..	1,860
June Quarter, 1866	..	2,230
September Quarter, 1866	600	2,515
March Quarter, 1867	..	3,559
September Quarter, 1867	..	3,286
1870	498	18,343
1875	803	30,008
1880	1,662	43,239
1885	2,595	64,635
1890	2,910	72,240
1895	2,903	60,802
1900	4,026	98,663
1901	4,165	105,242
1902	4,351	109,929
1903	4,402	107,671
1904	3,415*	102,597
1905	3,472	110,655
1906	3,666	118,555
1907	3,855	129,537
1908	3,891	126,759

* 1,000 non-purchasing members' names struck off.

APPENDIX.

BALANCE SHEET AS AT 5TH JUNE, 1909.

	£	s.	d.		£	s.	d.
Members' Shares	54,111	14	8	Stock-in-Trade	9,389	9	1
Interest due thereon	648	18	9	Properties, Fixed Stock, and Rolling Stock	26,320	0	0
Small Savings Bank	4,725	19	6	Clubs	188	5	8
Sundry Creditors for Goods	669	5	1	Secured Loans	4,024	4	5
General Reserve Fund	2,923	8	11	Loans	14,644	9	1
Dividend Reserve Fund	432	3	5	Shares	9,833	0	0
Insurance Fund	200	0	0	Cash	5,309	14	9
Jubilee Fund	603	18	3				
Balance Disposable	5,393	14	5				
	£69,709	3	0		£69,709	3	0

From the opening in 1859 to June, 1909:—

Sales £3,056,752
Dividend £396,960
Interest £50,025

Buildings, Fixtures, &c., written down from £52,890 to £26,320.

Co-operative Printing Society Limited, 118, Corporation Street, Manchester.

Milton Keynes UK
Ingram Content Group UK Ltd.
UKHW040637111224
3599UKWH00013B/68